Finding God

My Journey Through Pancreatic Cancer

Nick Seniour

Dedication

I dedicate this book to Karen, my wife of 59 years, and who has been by my side through better or worse, in sickness and health, richer or poorer, and was the stabilizing factor through my health journey. She was continually—literally—by my side.

Also our daughter, Chris Hunter that was my private nurse and counselor, coming every morning to hook up my IV and returned each afternoon to disconnect it. She and Karen encouraged me to eat when I didn't want to eat. Without these two I would not have been able to survive the journey as they constantly helped me carry the load.

I am thankful also to the numerous people that constantly knocked on heaven's door on my behalf.

I am also thankful to my personal physicians: Doctor Dohan, Doctor Troiano, Doctor House, and Doctor Ragavendra for all of your help in the process.

Finally, thank You Jesus that You saw fit to do the part that only You could do, for You extended my life from the original diagnosis of two to 18 months to only He knows. I shall ever be thankful that You extended my life.

Finding God: My Journey Through Pancreatic Cancer

Nick Seniour

Cover design: Vision Graphics, Seymour, IN

Printed in the United States of America

ISBN 978-0-9979146-2-7

Themes

Finding God: My Journey Through Pancreatic Cancer

My journey began with an unexpected conversation:

"Are you alright?"

"Yes, I think so."

"You're not alright. You're Jaundiced. Take off your glasses. Your eyes are yellow. You call your doctor, right now."

Since we had resigned as pastor from the last church we had planted in Aurora, Indiana, my wife Karen and I had both taken part-time jobs to keep us busy. We both worked in the same area, so we rode to work together. Karen, who was working a job at our church daycare facility, had gotten off work earlier than I and had come by to pick me up.

This authoritative voice in the opening dialog was Sarah, newly appointed boss for the trucking company where I was working. I later learned that Sarah was a retired nurse, and when she saw that I was very jaundiced, and knowing from her previous occupation as a nurse, she realized I had something serious going on.

Like an obedient son, I called Doctor Dohan, our personal doctor, and made an appointment to go to his office. Doctor Dohan is not only our doctor but also our friend. We had already been to the doctor and he had scheduled me to have an ultrasound. The results of the ultrasound hadn't shown any problems, but because I was now very jaundiced, he scheduled me to go to the hospital for a CT scan.

When doctor Dohan received the results of the CT scan, he called and told me he wanted me to come in to his office and discuss the results. The scan showed a small tumor on the tip of my pancreas. He said, "If this is cancer, it is in a very operable position for the Whipple surgery." This particular surgery is "a difficult and demanding operation and can have serious risks."[1] My response was why would I want to have a radical surgery at my age when all I have ever heard about pancreatic cancer is that if you get pancreatic cancer you are a dead man? Why would I want to torture my body with a radical surgery?

Doctor Dohan then made me an appointment with Doctor Troiano (gastroenterologist). This appointment was supposed to be for consultation, but the doctor took one look at me and said, "I am going to sweet talk the girls down in the operating room and try to get you in for a procedure this afternoon."

He then asked me what time I had eaten breakfast. I responded, "I had breakfast at 7:30 this morning." He said, "If anybody asks you, you had breakfast at 5:30. Do you understand? You had breakfast at 5:30."

That afternoon I was in the operating room to have a procedure and open my bile duct and take a biopsy to determine whether or not this tumor was cancerous. He then placed a stent in my bile duct, sent me to the recovery room, and finally sent me home. I told them not to send me home because I was very sick, but because of difficulties with my insurance company, they sent me home anyway.

After a very trying night, not being able to sleep because of how sick I was, the next morning I told Karen to take me back to the hospital. Upon arrival at the hospital the doctors told me that I had a "very angry pancreas" (whatever that means). They kept me in the hospital two more days and, not as yet having the results of the biopsy, told me that I very probably did have cancer.

Knowing the seriousness of having pancreatic cancer, and the very short life expectancy because of it, I decided to just pray and leave the final outcome to God. Having heard of the possibilities, and knowing the seriousness, I had no fear. I was a bundle of emotions but literally had no fear.

I prayed the prayer that Hezekiah prayed in the Old Testament:

> In those days was Hezekiah sick unto death. And Isaiah the prophet the son of Amoz came unto him, and said unto him, Thus says the Lord, Set thine house in order: for thou shalt die and not live. Then Hezekiah turned his face toward the wall, and prayed unto the Lord. And said, Remember now o Lord, I beseech thee, how I have walked before thee in truth and with a perfect heart, and have done that which is good in thy sight. and Hezekiah wept sore. Then came the word of the Lord to Isaiah saying, Go, and say to Hezekiah, Thus saith the Lord, the God of David thy father, I have heard thy prayer, I have seen thy tears: behold I will add unto thy days fifteen years. And I will deliver thee and this city out of the hand of the king of Assyyria: and I will defend this city. And this shall be a sign unto thee from the Lord, that the Lord will do this thing that he hath spoken; Behold I will bring again the shadow of degrees, which is gone down in the sundial of Ahaz, ten degrees backward. So the sun returned ten degrees, by which degrees it was gone down.
>
> Isaiah 38: 1–8

Is that an amazing story or is that an amazing story? Can you believe that the Lord not only promised that He was going to heal Hezekiah, but He was going to do something supernatural that had never been done before, or since, anywhere in the world, as a sign that He was going to do what He said He would do. It was an unheard of, impossible thing that happened.

Do you think Hezekiah had any doubt that God would do what He said He would do? Hezekiah must have had faith to believe that God could heal him or he would have never prayed. Can you imagine how he felt when that sun dial began to move backward? In my calculations, ten degrees would amount to about thirty minutes on a modern day clock.

If the Word of God is true, and I believe it is because the Bible says that God cannot lie, then in Acts10:34, it says that God is no respecter of persons. If that be the case, we can expect God to do the supernatural in our lives. God is not just a God of miracles in the Bible, He is a modern day miracle worker. The same God that walked on water can also walk all over the things in your life that have overwhelmed you.

In Mark 9:23 Jesus declares, "If you can believe, all things are possible to him that believeth." He didn't say some things are possible, He said all things. In my mind, if He said all things, He meant all things. You say, but the doctor said my problem is terminal. I know what the doctor said, but what did God say? I am not putting the doctor down. He is saying and doing what he has been trained to do. He spent many years learning about sicknesses and cures for certain sicknesses. But rest assured the doctor does not have the last word. Life and death are in the big powerful hands of God.

My pastor, when I was a child, said we will pray for the sick, and if God doesn't heal them, they need to get the best doctor they can find. I have quoted that many times, but as I was writing this, I believe the Lord said to me that if you say that, you have given that person an easy option. Well, if God doesn't heal me in the next five minutes, I am going straight to the hospital.

I am not against hospitals and doctors; actually, I am very thankful for them, but I don't allow myself to put all of my trust in a doctor when I have found, by experience, that God is a healer. He is—as the song says—a way maker, miracle worker, and promise keeper.[2] And he is My God. I have chosen Him to be my personal God.

After praying Hezekiah's prayer, I just laid back on my hospital bed to rest and meditate on God. A little while later Pastor Tony Oliver rolled into my room, on a knee scooter because of a ruptured Achilles tendon. He had no more than gotten in my room that he began to speak prophetically. He proclaimed, "Elder, it is not over, you are going to make it through this. God is not finished with you yet!" Tony then said, "As I was headed over here today, the Lord quickened the words of Hezekiah's prayer to my mind, and it's not over." I said, "I accept that."

Don't tell me that there is no God. Do you think that Tony's proclamation of healing was just something he had made up? I hardly think so. Is it just a coincidence that he spoke the exact words to me that I had just prayed? I believe God gave him those words to confirm what I had just prayed.

Don't tell me that God does not hear and answer prayer today. I choose to believe that God heard my prayer, and I am so thankful that He is still a prayer answering God. I am so thankful for all of His many blessings in my life. I am so thankful He cares so much that He would send someone to speak encouragement to me in my time of need.

Later that afternoon, one of the doctors came in and asked how I was doing. I don't really remember how I responded, but it was probably something like the following. "I am doing okay Doc, for the shape I am in." He then said, "I don't think we have the results of the biopsy from your procedure."

The nurse was sitting there looking at her computer and said, "I think the results are here." The doctor looked at the results and walked back to my bed side and looked me in the eye and simply said, "Oh, yes it is cancer." I am so happy that the Lord had other plans, and His plan for this time was not cancer!

I asked him, "What does that mean?" He said, "Without treatment you probably have two months and with treatment maybe a year and a half." I never had any real fear, but my mind went into overdrive trying to figure out how I would complete all of the things I needed to get done if this was, in fact, the end for me. However, I could not bring myself to believe this was the end, and having Pastor Tony Oliver's prophetic words to hold on to, I just couldn't bring myself to accept that this was the end.

Cleaning Out

They discharged me from the hospital on Saturday. I had prayed that God would give me some time to set my personal house in order, so I immediately made a phone call to a man who the previous year had been interested in purchasing my shop property and the rental house that was also on the same property. Sunday afternoon he and his wife were at our house and bought that property.

I then started a series of five high power chemotherapy treatments. Along with the diagnosis of cancer came COVID-19. It was my plan to have an auction sale to dispose of the 30 years of contents of the shop, but due to everything being shut down because of the COVID-19 pandemic, we were not able to have an auction. Then, because we couldn't have an auction and because the shop was on a state highway, I decided I would just put out a sign advertising a tool sale. Because of everything being shut down, there was hardly any traffic on the highway. However, a few people did stop by and bought a few items. Because of the lack of traffic, I started giving things away to friends who would stop in. I wanted my sons to have my tools, but neither of them had room for them. Fortunately, with the occasional help of my son Scott and my brother, we finally got the shop cleaned out, except for my very large tool box and large commercial air compressor. Time was running out, and I needed to get these things moved because I was going to have surgery the next week.

Sunday afternoon Karen and I were sitting at home. Churches had been closed because of COVID. While sitting there trying to figure out how to accomplish moving these items, I told Karen that I was going to the shop and figure out how to, at least, move my tool box. Karen sad, "If you are going I am going with you." We went to the shop and rolled my large tool box over to the lift, hooked some straps on it and lifted it up, then backed my trailer under it and set it on the trailer.

We then loaded the larger bottom roller cabinet the same way. When we got to the house I just rolled the heavy lower tool chest off of the trailer. Now to get the top half off. I unloaded it with a hoist called a cherry picker. The cherry picker got it almost high enough to set it on the bottom part but not quite. I had Karen push forward on the cherry picker as I pushed up as high as I could. Now she gave a hard push forward, and I heaved a final time and finally got the tool chest together.

I told the man who bought the shop that I was not able to get the air compressor moved. He said "I will have my help pick it up with our Bob Cat and bring it over and set it in place." So the next day they moved the air compressor and man-handled it into place. Thank God for friends.

Surgery

We had to go back to our family doctor, Doctor Dohan, for some medicine changes. COVID had now kicked into high gear. When we arrived at the doctor's office we were the only patients in his office. When the doctor came in he asked, "Why haven't you considered the Whipple surgery?" I responded, "At my age (77), why would I want to torture my body with a radical surgery, when there is no cure for pancreatic cancer?"

He got up from his computer and walked out of the room. A few minutes later he returned with information about the Whipple surgery and handed it to both Karen and me. While we were reading, he picked up the phone and called Doctor House at IU Health Hospital who specializes in the Whipple surgery procedure. Because there were no other patients in the office, Dr. Dohan spent 3 ½ hours with us, and when we left his office that day, I was scheduled to meet Doctor House the following week.

During this process, so far, I had no fear, even though I was given plenty of negative information, but when I awoke on the day of my appointment with Doctor House, I was troubled with whether or not I should go ahead with surgery. When I prayed that morning I told the Lord that when we are at Doctor House's office, if he says one negative word, I am not going to have surgery.

We arrived at the hospital and were directed to an examination room. Chris, our daughter who is a registered nurse, went with us to be an extra set of ears and sounding board as we made our decisions. What a blessing she has been during this whole process. Thank God for her wisdom and experience as we journeyed down this untraveled road.

The nurse came in to gather our information. After about thirty minutes Doctor House came in, sat down on his little roller stool, rolled over to me, looked me in the eye, and said, "I have looked over your information, and you are a perfect candidate for the Whipple surgery, maybe even a cure!" Not one negative word. Surgery was scheduled for June 16, 2020.

Because of the COVID pandemic, they told us I could not have anyone with me in the hospital: no visitors! On the day of surgery Karen could come and sit in the waiting room. After surgery was over they would give her the results, and then she would have to leave and not come back until I was ready to be released. That was going to be a rough time, me in a lonely, barren hospital room, all by myself for what would turn out to be two weeks. BUT GOD had other plans, and on Monday, the day before my surgery on Tuesday, the hospital relaxed the restrictions and Karen was able to be with me. She drove thirty-five miles every day, except one, the two weeks I was in the hospital. She needed one day to stay at home and get some work done, and our son Nick drove up from Kentucky the day she didn't make it. Thank God for family.

Surgery day arrived, and we made our way to IU Medical Facility in Indianapolis to proceed as planned. I had been told before surgery that they judged the cancer to be stage 4, which is not a number you really would want to have. Surgery was successful as Doctor House removed a little part of my pancreas having a small stage one tumor. They also removed twelve lymph nodes of which none had any cancer. Thank You Jesus! (Just for the record, if you have noticed, I have never taken ownership of cancer. It is not my cancer). I am a believer that we need to speak positive words.

After they removed the twelve lymph nodes, I had a rare condition called a chyle leak, which sometimes happens after surgery. Due to this chyle leak, there was a build-up of fluid in my stomach which required a stomach drain tube. In order to treat the chyle leak, I had to have a no fat diet. My diet consisted of foods such as dry sliced turkey, green beans with no seasoning, white potatoes in the can, pretzels, etc. I was weary with my diet, and Karen was weary trying to prepare it. The dietician told her that we couldn't eat anything other than what she prepared, because we didn't know what was in it. We were also weary dealing with the chyle leak. We had to keep a record of how much liquid this leak was producing each day. In order to get rid of the drain, it had to be down to 20 ml per day. It was still producing 400 ml per day and not coming down very quickly.

When I came home from the hospital, I needed to have an IV for a few weeks to keep me hydrated and have some nutrition. Chris, our daughter that is a registered nurse, came to our house two times every day to hook up the IV and to disconnect it. She would also coax me to eat, but I was weary of the diet. I was very frustrated one day and told Karen, "Drive me over to Franklin and drive around Freddy's hamburger restaurant and at least let me smell it." Of course we didn't do it, but that was how I felt.

Searching For God

Since we were dealing with the food situation and no in-house church, along with all of the concerns about COVID, I had somewhat settled into a state of depression. I am usually pretty upbeat, but this particular evening I became overwhelmed with our circumstances. I was sitting in my chair, and as Karen walked by, I stopped her and said, "I feel like the Lord is so far away. He is so far away I don't even know where He is. I need to hear His voice. Oh, if I could only find Him! If I could just get a word!"

I want you to understand the fact that God is much larger and more capable than we may ever think or believe. Finding God is a real possibility, and when He shows up, there is nothing that will be too large for Him to handle. If you are searching for God you must believe it is possible to find Him.

I believe there are many times when God speaks to us, but because of the fact that we are always so busy, we are not close enough to Him to be able to hear when He speaks. I have come to the conclusion that God speaks regularly, but we are simply not spiritually prepared to hear what He is saying.

Because of my dream encounter with God, I have found that I desire to live in a spiritual realm where, when He speaks, I can readily discern His voice. I want to have that type of relationship with God.

There is an old song that says "He walks with me and he talks with me, and he tells me I am his own, and the joy we share as we tarry there, none other has ever known."[3] Oh, what a joy to be in the presence of royalty! Our King is different than an earthly king. He is the answer to anything that we need. What a joy it is to live your life in the presence of the King of Glory!

If you truly desire to find God in your time of need, it is good to have a relationship with God. You may feel that you can never get good enough to get God. That is true. You will never get good enough to get God, you have to get God to get good. God is not looking for perfection, He is looking for a heart that is desperately searching for Him. He is looking for someone that has a strong desire to know Him. He is looking for someone that will love Him and submit to His will regardless of what that may be.

It is good to have a relationship with God for your sake and not His. God will come to you when you   draw near to Him. The Scripture declares: "Draw nigh to God, and he will draw nigh to you. Cleanse your hands ye sinners; and purify your hearts, ye double minded" (James 4:8).

The first part of this Scripture simply tells us to draw closer to God. The rest of this Scripture suggests that if we are not serving God, or have spiritual issues and want to come near to God, we need to clean up our act by repentance.

Another translation of this Scriptures says: "Come close to God and He will come close to you. [Recognize that you are] sinners, get your soiled hands clean; [realize that you have been disloyal] wavering individuals with divided interests, and purify your hearts [of your spiritual adultery]" (James 4: 8 Amplified Bible).

You may be in the middle of the worst situation of your life and feel like there is no hope and no one to help you, but if you will turn your face toward God and call on Him and open up your heart to Him, He says, "I will hear, I will be available, I will answer, and I will help you."

When you begin to open your heart to God, you must believe that what He said in His Word, He will do. It takes the element of faith to come to God and plead your case and expect God to look at your case. You may say, "I am not ready to do that. I enjoy doing the things I do and living my life the way I want to live." I hardly think that is the way you feel or you would have never purchased this book to begin with.

I hope I am not too abrupt with the above statements, but if you truly are searching for God, whether it be for healing or you just want to have a closer relationship with God, it will cost you something. All through the Bible, God's people have always been a special people. God's people have always been different than those who don't know Him or don't have a relationship with Him.

There are some things that God's people do not do. There are some places God's people don't go. There are certain attitudes they don't have. The instruction book for those who are trying to live for God is the good old Bible. It pretty much covers everything that God expects from His people.

Finding God: My Journey Through Pancreatic Cancer

Believe it or not, regardless of what anyone thinks, regardless of what the schools teach, there is still a heaven, and there is still a hell. Heaven will still be a place of great beauty, great peace, and a place that has no room for anything that God has declared off-limits. The beauties of heaven will be so great that we will be amazed just to look at that wonderful place.

Hell is still a place for bad people, and contrary to popular opinion, there will also be good people there who did not surrender their lives to God.

The Bible gives numerous bits of instruction to let us know what is right and what is wrong. I am not super spiritual, but I have chosen to live my life according to the Word of God and not take any chances on missing out on what I have lived my life for.

You don't need to be embarrassed to acknowledge your need for God. I have been a pastor and church planter (someone who starts new churches) for over thirty-five years. Sometimes the pastor (preacher) goes through the same tests and trials as everyone else. Sometimes he faces the same health issues as everyone else. Just because he is the preacher doesn't make him immune to problems with his health just like everyone else.

Let me just throw in a Scripture to support some of my previous statements. Galatians 5:19–21 gives a whole list of things that God considers sin. Verse 21 finishes up by saying, "they which do such things (the things listed in the preceding verses—even if you don't know what these words mean) shall not inherit the kingdom of God."

These are some pretty strong Scriptures, and if I was trying to find God, I would get a good Bible dictionary and find out what the words mean.

In my situation I had come through Whipple surgery for pancreatic cancer. Not one time had I requested for God to heal me. I had asked Him for a space of time to set my house in order. When I left the hospital—after being there two weeks after surgery—I came home to five weeks of circumstances that brought me to the place where I felt like God was nowhere to be found. As I stated before, I am not a person who gets depressed easily, but I found myself depressed because of all the circumstances I was experiencing. That was when I told my wife Karen, "I feel like the Lord is so far away. He's so far away I don't even know where He is. I need to hear his voice. Oh, if I could just find Him. If I could just get a word from God!"

That was when I began my journey to find Him. I wasn't praying for healing or anything else in particular. I just wanted to be able to feel His presence. If you want to find God, seek His face and not His hand. If you get His face you will have His hand. In my case I got a miracle! I got rid of a stomach tube and bag, and Karen and I got to eat our first diet of normal food after five weeks of a no fat diet. The icing on the cake was when Doctor House pronounced that I had beaten pancreatic cancer. The statistic for beating pancreatic cancer is 1%. I am so glad I was able to find God!

Finding God

That night I made up my mind that I was going on a quest. I was going to do everything in my power to be sensitive enough to hear His voice. I have to find him. I must have His direction. My life will be so empty and void if I can't find Him. Here I am cancer free, but my life will not be worth living if I can't find God. Why can't I find Him? Why can't I even feel His touch? Where is He?

I felt like Job: "Oh that I knew where I might find him! That I might come even to his seat" (Job 23: 3). I began to look through the Scriptures and try to find some clue as to why I wasn't able to find God.

Finding God: My Journey Through Pancreatic Cancer

Jesus said, "If thou canst believe, all things are possible to him that believeth" (Mark 9:23). We say we believe but fail to have the fruit of our belief in our hand. We need to live a life of expectation and believe that God is working things out. I have come to believe that God is speaking to us on a regular basis, but we fail to hear what He is saying because we are focused on everything else. Occasionally we get into a situation that causes us real stress or pain. Then we check in with God, but our main focus is on self.

Jesus said, "If any man have ears to hear, let him hear" (Mark 4: 23). (He didn't say, "If any man have ears, let him hear;" rather, He said, "If any man have ears to hear, let him hear.") We have ears that hear a lot of things, but if you want to hear God you will need to have a keen appetite for His voice. You also need to be able to recognize His voice when He speaks.

I was on a journey to find God. Nothing else mattered, I had to find God. My mind was made up, my ears were listening, my heart was fixed, my eyes were focused, and I intended to find God. Nothing is going to get in my way. I don't care what anyone thinks, nothing satan says is going to hinder me. This is between me and God. (In the last book I wrote, *It's Not About Me, A life about Him,* I talk about how we live and direct our lives.) But in this situation it was about my relationship with God. It is when you come to the place in your life that nothing or no one else matters, God shows up.

I began to search my heart. I repented of anything that might possibly be in my way of finding God. Literally, nothing else mattered. It was get out of my way or I will run over you to find the One that my soul loves, because I knew that all things would change when God showed up. Never in my lifetime was there a time when I could not find God. And now when I was facing some of the worst challenges of my life, it felt as though there was not even a slight breeze blowing in the spiritual world. I have come to the conclusion that, spiritually, we all need a life threatening situation in our lives. It is during these times that our faith boils to the top of the pan and runs over. The Apostle Peter wrote:

> Wherein ye greatly rejoice, though now for a season, if need be, ye are in heaviness through manifold temptations: That the trial of your faith, being much more precious than of gold that perisheth, though it be tried with fire, that it might be found unto praise and honor and glory at the appearing of Jesus Christ:
>
> I Peter 1: 6-7

For me, life would not be worth living without Christ in my life. My whole being depends on having Christ in my life. I don't know how anyone can live without Jesus, the one that I love, living in their life.

It was with that mindset that I went to sleep on the evening of June 20, 2020. However, at 6:30 in the morning of June 21, I had a dream that would ultimately change my life. As I said earlier, we had been dealing with some very disheartening situations, my wife trying to prepare increasingly difficult meals, and a stomach drain producing 400 ml of fluid a day and was not dropping down to 20 ml per day in order to be removed. My search to find God had, so far, not been successful.

I knew if I could find God, at least my spirit would be lifted because of the many times He had brought help in our times of need. Our family was no stranger to health adversities. As a child, maybe four years old, I remember riding in the car, bringing my dad home from the hospital after he had been healed of an extremely serious sickness. (More on that in another chapter.)

It was 6:30 in the morning on July 21, 2020 that I heard from God. No, He never spoke to me in the way that I would have imagined.

Finding God: My Journey Through Pancreatic Cancer

I did not hear a booming, bass voice, but regardless, if it was not in the way that I would have expected, it was without a doubt a word from the Lord. I was so sure that this dream had significance that I wrote down the time that it appeared.

In my dream I was somehow on an upper floor on the outside of a large concrete commercial building. I assumed this was a church building. A door opened, and there was a large group of people sitting inside what appeared to be a Sunday School class. There were two or three Apostolic ladies walking back and forth on the sidewalk in front of the building.

Beside my office door I have a sign that reads "all things are possible." I can see this sign while I am sitting at my desk or when I walk out the door. I made this sign one evening a few years ago while I was praying and studying and my faith was running high. Since it reminds me every time I am in my office that all things are possible, it helps me to keep in mind that ALL THINGS ARE POSSIBLE WITH GOD!

I have never forgotten, not even for one minute, that all things are, indeed, possible when we bring God into the equation. Sorry, but I can't go any farther without expounding a little more on the fact that I wholeheartedly believe that God can do anything!

There is nothing too big for God. There is nothing too small for God. There is nothing too wide for God. There is nothing too out of control for God. There is absolutely nothing God cannot do. As human beings we are apt to focus more on our problems than we do on the problem solver. (More on miracles later.)

Back to my dream. One of the ladies walking on the sidewalk looked up at me and said, "You are going to be preaching in a little while." I responded, "No, that won't happen. It won't happen because before

I preach I always pray about what to preach, and I haven't prayed about that. Also, before I preach I always put some effort and study into it, and I haven't studied about it. So, there is absolutely no possibility that I will be preaching." She looked up at me, shaking her finger at me and yelled, "NOTHING IS IMPOSSIBLE WITH GOD!"

By now it is 6:45 in the morning, and when she said nothing is impossible with God, I sat straight up in bed, and pointing my finger back at her, said, "You're right. That's mine. That's for me, and I accept it. Nothing is impossible with God."

When Karen woke up a little while later, I said to her, "It's over." She asked, "What's over?" I pointed to the drainage tube and the bag on my side and said, "This stupid thing and you having to fix these dumb meals. I can't explain how it's going to be over, I just know that this situation is about to end."

Doubt said, "But you still have the drainage tube and the bag on your side, and Karen is going to prepare the same no-fat meal today." Faith said, "I don't know how it's going to happen, but it will happen." For the next two days the drainage tube still produced 400 ml of fluid each day. Those same two days we still had the same no-fat diet, but it was different now because I knew that somehow and some way it was over.

Two days after my dream I went to IU Hospital to meet the surgeon for my five week postop appointment. Since we could not eat at a restaurant, Karen packed us a little snack of sliced turkey, pickles, and some pretzels. (Doesn't that sound appetizing?) As we were walking down the hall to an examination room, I saw my surgeon, Doctor House, sitting in a little side room working on his computer. As I passed by, I pulled up my shirt, clasped the stomach tube, and began to swing it at him. He just smiled as we walked by.

Finding God: My Journey Through Pancreatic Cancer

We were directed into an examination room, and in a few minutes another doctor from Doctor House's group came in and asked a lot of questions. She then left, and in a little while Doctor House came in, along with the other doctor. Doctor House said, "Get up here on this table. That tube is coming out today." Remember, we are in the hospital. I raised both of my arms as high as I could raise them and yelled at the top of my voice, "HALLELUJAH!" Karen was sitting over in the corner, and she was saying "Thank you Jesus" and worshiping our great big Savior.

I said to the doctor, "So the tube is coming out today?" Then I was questioning how that could be when I am still producing 400 ml of fluid each day. He was trying to give me some kind of explanation of why the tube could come out. It didn't make sense to me, but the tube was coming out. Hallelujah!

I then asked him what I could eat. He said, "You can eat anything you want. If you have a problem with something, give it a little time and try it again." I told him the story about me telling Karen to take me to Freddy's and drive around it and let me just smell it. We had a little laugh, and I then said, "Freddy's, here we come."

I then asked him what I could do. I wanted to get off of the porch and out of the chair and go to work. He said, "You can do whatever you feel like doing," I said, "Great, I need to mow three acres of grass this afternoon." That afternoon I was on my Dixie Chopper and mowed about half of the yard and finished it the next day.

Now the other doctor was removing the stomach tube and stitching me up. I was paying attention to her because I was feeling the pain from her needle. Doctor House turned to Karen and said, "Your husband is a very fortunate man to BEAT pancreatic cancer."

Thank God for all the doctors do, but we know, ultimately, healing is up to Jesus by Whose stripes we are healed.

Recognizing God

The result of me finding God came from a dream. No, I didn't see God, but in the dream I saw God the way He chose for me to see Him, and without a doubt I heard from God. No, like I said before, it wasn't a booming, deep bass voice. This voice happened to belong to a lady who at that time and moment became God's messenger to speak to me. When she spoke, she spoke with authority. When she said, "Nothing is impossible with God," I knew at that moment she was speaking as a messenger from God. This was what I had been praying for.

I bought into the concept that this was, in fact, the voice of the Lord speaking to me. When she said, "Nothing is impossible with God," it really rang a bell in my spirit. My thought was, this is what I have been praying for. God has visited our house to deliver a message to me personally, confirming what I already knew. He confirmed that nothing is impossible with Him! This was also the answer to my prayer just to be able to feel God and experience a restoration in my spirit that God was still present and available when I searched for Him with all of my heart.

God really had no choice but to show up, for the Bible tells us that God cannot lie. His Word says in Jeremiah 29:13, "And ye shall seek me, and find me, when ye shall search for me with all your heart." Oh, I love the sound of that!

I was searching for Him with all of my heart, so He had no choice but to show up. You may think I am being a little bit on the crazy side. I am not a little bit on the crazy side, I am a whole lot crazy about Jesus. He is my Savior, my help in the time of trouble, and my defender when satan comes against me. He has proven that He is my

Finding God: My Journey Through Pancreatic Cancer

healer, and I will live as long as He says so.

This situation had been going on for five weeks and not making any progress. Naturally speaking, I had no reason to believe that anything was going to change any time soon. Be assured, God knows what is going on in your life, and He is concerned about it. The great King of the whole universe is concerned about you personally.

> For we have not an high priest which cannot be touched with the feeling of our infirmities; but was in all points tempted like as we are, yet without sin.
>
> Hebrews 4: 15

You may say, "I prayed, and God never answered my prayer, so I am just going to give up on God." When you pray, you must have faith that God is going to do something about your situation. He may not answer your prayer the way you prayed it, because sometimes your prayer may not be according to His will. Some things we pray for may not be good for us, and God knows ahead of time if what we are praying for is going to be good for us.

As I mentioned before, my prayer was not for healing. I prayed that if this was the end for me that it would be alright. Three doctors had suggested that without treatment I might have two months. With treatment I might (notice the wording—might) have a year and a half. I was good with whatever God chose for me, I just wanted Him to give me time to get some personal things in order to make it easier for my wife after putting up with me for fifty nine years.

I never begged for anything. The truth is I was ready to accept His perfect will for my life. If His will meant the graveyard—although I really didn't want to go there yet—I was ready to make the crossing. The title of my first book says it well, *It's Not About Me, A life about Him*, and that is still my feeling today.

Because I was willing to accept God's will, He gave me a bonus. He gave me two CT scans that said there was no cancer in my body. I have always been a man of faith, and today I am more a man of faith than ever before.

While sitting here thinking about how good the Lord is, I am reminded of an old song. It goes something like this:

> He's sweet I know, He's sweet I know. Storm clouds may rise, strong winds may blow, but I'll tell the world wherever I go, that I have found a savior, and He's sweet I know.[4]

That is the kind of God I have been serving all these years. He has been so good to me that I have absolutely no complaint. He doesn't just come along every time I whimper, but He has never failed me when I am in trouble. He is the Lord of my life and I don't have any desire to change that.

Speak Faith

This whole journey has been a journey of faith. As children of God we need to also be people of faith. Faith means that we speak positive. There are times when we all have a negative thought, but we should never let negative words come out of our mouths. How can we have positive results to our prayers if we are speaking negatively?

I am not one to moan and groan or complain. I have found, through many difficult life experiences, that God is so good that I would never ever want to accuse Him or speak negatively toward Him. I have found through the years that God has never done me anything but good. I don't know how you "really" perceive God, but I see Him as nothing but good.

Finding God: My Journey Through Pancreatic Cancer

If you choose to see Him negatively or accuse Him, you can't expect Him to do good things for you. Proverbs 18: 21 tells us that "Death and life are in the power of the tongue." If you don't believe it, you will never see it. If you want God's healing hand in your life, you need to be able to visualize yourself well, healed by the power of God.

I was at a certain church one time and a lady stood up to testify. I have no idea how she thought she was testifying. I thought a testimony was expressing the goodness of the Lord or perhaps something wonderful that had happened, and you knew God had performed it. However, as this dear sister opened her mouth, she was talking about trying to get her family to come to church, and she said, "The only way you can get people to come to church is to bring them in a hearse."

My thoughts were maybe they knew if they came she was going to say something like that, and they were not interested in being embarrassed. (Be careful little—or big—tongue what you say.) I have heard people say my kids will never come to church. You're right, they probably never will, because you don't even have a little bit of faith that they will ever darken the doors of a church. If that is your mindset, how are you able to pray for them?

I know it is discouraging for you when you see your children away from God, but when you pray, you need to visualize your children coming through the church door and falling on their face at an altar and making up their mind to serve God.

My Dad

The above thoughts remind me of my dad's story. Due to his mother's death, when he was six months old, he was raised by his grandparents. His family was some of the first ones to accept the

29

truth of Jesus Name baptism in the early 1900's. He grew up in the church, but in his teen years he decided that he would do his own thing, so he left the church. As is usually the case, he got involved with the wrong crowd and picked up some bad habits.

Since he was raised by his godly grandparents, their hearts were very heavy because of his waywardness, so they continually prayed that he would return to the ways of the Lord. Never was there ever a negative word suggesting that "Lee boy" was hopeless. In their minds he was going to be saved.

Although he was away from the Lord, his family continued to pray for "Lee boy" to return to his roots. Later he married my mother, who was a committed Christian, and she also picked up the burden to pray for her backslidden husband that he would change his ways.

I was too young to realize what was going on, but when dad would come home drunk after a night out with the boys, mom would be very gentle with him. She would get him cleaned up and help him get into his night clothes. Then she would pray for him as she gently helped him get into bed. Not one time did she berate him or tell him how awful he was.

Dad respected mom and would never harm her or treat her badly. She just kept praying for him and believing that God was going to answer her prayer. You never know how God is going to answer, but faith says I know that He will answer.

Dad had a boil on his nose, and he decided that he was going to squeeze it and try to get some relief from the pain it was causing. Because of his squeezing, it became infected. After trying to self-medicate, he ended up in the hospital with a very serious condition called cavernous sinus thrombosis, having a blood and infection clot behind one eye. Those were the days before powerful antibiotics were readily available, so there was really no way to treat his situation. His condition deteriorated to the place where he lay there unconscious for thirteen days.

Those were also the days of party line phones and telegrams, so his family began to phone long distance and telegram all of their family and church members whom they knew all across the United States. This created a prayer chain that never stopped petitioning God on behalf of "Lee boy," interceding for his very life.

Dad told me that he knew he was dying. He was in the hospital in Indianapolis. Occasionally he would awaken only to drift very quickly back into unconsciousness. He said, "I knew I was dying because when I awoke one time for a few minutes, I saw my aunt from California sitting in a chair beside my bed. I would then drift off again, and when I woke up again, another aunt from Cleveland was there." Ironically, the two aunts that he saw sitting there were not people who would pray. The church continued to pray even when the doctor said he was going to die. The doctors continued to treat him to the best of their ability, but they told my mom that "She was an awfully young lady to be a widow." Meanwhile, the family and the church did what they believed would bring the results. They prayed without ceasing:

> Is any among you afflicted? Let him pray. Is any merry?
> Let him sing psalms. Is any sick among you? Let him
> call for the elders of the church; and let them pray over
> him, anointing him with oil in the name of the Lord.
> And the prayer of faith shall save the sick, and the
> Lord shall raise him up; and if he hath committed sins,
> they shall be forgiven him. Confess your faults one to
> another, that ye may be healed. The effectual fervent
> prayer of a righteous man availeth much.
>
> James 5: 13-16

Prayer for dad continued. On the 13th day he opened his eyes and looked around. His aunt was sitting in the chair beside his bed. When she saw that he was awake, she asked him if she could get anything for him. He answered saying, "I am hungry." That doesn't surprise me because dad was always hungry. His aunt then asked what he would like to eat. He said, "I would like to have a piece of cherry pie." I guess that runs in the family. I am always ready for a piece of Karen's cherry pie.

His aunt then decided that she would get him some cherry pie, knowing that when she came back he would have lapsed back into unconsciousness. She ran out the door of his hospital room, down the stairway, out the door, across the street to the restaurant, and got a piece of cherry pie. Back across the street, through the door, and then she ran up the stairs and back into his room.

Much to her surprise "Lee boy" was awake and sitting up in bed, with his mouth watering as he waited for his cherry pie. He was immediately transformed from a living dead man to a vibrant living man, cheating the mortician out of a sale.

The doctors realized there had, indeed, been a great miracle. However, they were not going to let go so quickly. They had previously told mom that if dad lived, his eye had been damaged so badly—being swollen almost out of his head—that he would not be able to see out of that eye.

After a few days dad went to the eye doctor who told him that he had a set of eyes that they read about in the text book but had never seen in the office. Let me be very bold and tell you that I have seen many miracles, and God is still alive and well and in the healing business. Don't let anyone tell you that the day of miracles is over. I still believe that the Bible is true, and Jesus Christ is the same yesterday, today, and forever.

Finding God: My Journey Through Pancreatic Cancer

Dad's hospital stay was the game changer in his life. No longer did he visit the bar room with his buddies on Saturday evening and need mom's help getting cleaned up and in bed. Now, instead of playing golf on Sunday morning, he was going to church and taking—not sending—his family to church on Sunday, Tuesday, Thursday, and any other time the doors of the church were open.

No longer did mom have to wonder where he was. He was at work, at home, or at church. If I happened to walk into their bedroom when it was bed time, I would see my dad kneeling beside his bed talking to his Friend, the one who had changed his life. His life changed so drastically that it wasn't long before he was asked to serve on the deacon board of his church, and later he served as head deacon. His life was now about Christ.

He had no ministerial training but, after a while, our pastor asked him if he would teach an out-of-control boy's Sunday School class. Our church was on a not-so-nice and deteriorating side of town. The young men were not bad guys but extremely mischievous and just plain ornery. The first Sunday dad taught, he entered the class and these boys decided that they would give him some of the same medicine they had given the previous teacher. He then let them know they were going to be under a different administration now. He said, "I want you to know that they didn't ask me to take this class because I am a good teacher. They appointed me to keep order and that is what I am going to do." He told them the things they were used to doing were now unacceptable. "You will not be chewing gum. Your chair will, at all times, have four legs on the floor, no leaning back on two legs. Throwing paper wads would not be tolerated, and no talking back and forth while I am teaching, and if you choose to reject these guidelines, you will be excused to go and sit in the pastor's class."

The first few weeks these boys decided that they were going to test this new teacher and see if his bite was as bad as his growl. One of the first tests was when the pastor's son decided that he was above the law and disobeyed this new inexperienced teacher. After a couple warnings, he was sent out to be a student in his father's adult class. Of course, he was noticed, and after that he decided to abide by the new teacher's rules. Doing so was a lot better that being a spectacle in his dad's class.

There was a large and very stout young man named Mickey who was quite respected among his peers. Although he was not serving the Lord, he took a liking to my dad. One Sunday another young man decided it was his turn to test his luck with the teacher. He leaned his chair back on two legs. Dad told him to sit his chair down on all four legs. He continued to talk and lean his chair back. Mickey turned around and told him, "You do what the man said." The four legs of his chair immediately dropped with a thud back on the floor, and these few incidents established law and order in that class.

By this time dad realized that to do a good job he needed to really get into God's Word. He was given Sunday School literature, which he used, but he didn't just use that. He would pray and study, over and above the literature he was given, and He became a very talented Bible teacher.

The atmosphere in this once challenging class had changed completely, and now it was time to move on to greater things. Dad was asked if he would mind if they combined the boy's class and the girl's class, which became a great success. If I were to be introduced to a stranger by one of his students today, I would invariably be introduced, no matter how many years ago it had been, as "his dad was my Sunday School teacher." Dad, along with my mother, at a later time planted a new church. Not bad for an eighth grade school dropout.

Finding God: My Journey Through Pancreatic Cancer

When God spoke healing to my dad there was a real life change that came with it. It was because of dad's spiritual experience that he dove headlong into the work of God to start a new church. Then, because he started the church, it challenged me to a life of ministry when I was in my thirties. Two new churches and two troubled churches later I am still searching and praying for God's direction for my life.

The progression continues with our two sons. Nick went into the ministry and now pastors a thriving church in Kentucky. Scott has been the pastor of one church, and after resigning from that position, became an assistant pastor of a large Indiana church for eight years and is now in the process of praying for God to open the door so he can step back into the role of a pastor. We are very supportive of our two sons that have followed our lead and picked up the ministry mantle.

Besides the ministry on our side of the family, my sister's son, Jeff, went into the ministry and pioneered an awesome church. Jeff also has some very probable ministers coming along behind him, all because one man and his wife committed their lives to service in God's Kingdom. What could God do through you if you made a total commitment to His cause?

This can all be traced back to the fact that W. Lee Seniour listened to God and chose to turn from his wayward ways and follow the leading of the Lord. I am so happy that God has chosen to allow our family to continue the trend of ministry. God only knows what can happen in your family if you will simply choose to serve God with all of your heart.

It is amazing what you can do after you hear the Lord speak. When they told me I had anywhere from two months to a year and a half to live, something like a fire was kindled in my heart. Nothing else really matters except what I can still accomplish for my Jesus. I pray regularly, "Lord, what would you have me do?" I have chosen to hear and respond to His still small voice.

After the pronouncement of my life expectancy, I continue to live with the same priorities as before. God must be number one, my wife and family are second. I have no regrets as to my priorities for my life. I simply love serving Jesus. He has been better to me than anyone or anything in my life. I challenge you to choose Jesus! At the time of this writing it has been eight months since I was given a death warrant. I have long bypassed the two month date and looking much farther ahead than the 1 ½ year mark. I am looking forward a few more years with great expectation about where the will of God will take me. Hallelujah!

I wrote the previous paragraph on Friday, December 4, 2020, after having a CT scan the day before. Today is Monday, December 7. At 11:20 this morning I was at my oncologist, Doctor Raghavendras office, to find out the results from Thursday's CT scan. The scan covered my chest, abdomen, and pelvis. When she entered the examination room I told her I was expecting a good report today. She said, "How does the word remission sound?" I got up and did a little dance around the room, thanking Jesus.

We then told her that when I had to go back to the hospital after having a chemotherapy treatment, the doctor there told us, after I had a CT scan, that only one percent of those having pancreatic cancer survive. She agreed that only around one percent survive. I am sitting here at my computer this evening with tears of joy and thanksgiving rolling down my cheeks for what God has seen fit to do for me.

A great big thank you goes to Doctor Dohan for his role in finding the problem, and to Doctor Troiano, Doctor House, and Doctor

Finding God: My Journey Through Pancreatic Cancer

Raghavenda for all that you have done during this process. Ultimately my thanksgiving and praise goes to my wonderful friend, Jesus Christ, for the stripes He received that paid for my healing before He submitted to Calvary's cross.

Miracles

Over the years I owned an excavating business. The major part of our business for years was the installation of septic systems. Later, I moved out of that phase of business to the digging of footings and installation of water and sewer lines for companies building production homes. It was fast paced and provided me a living so I could work doing my first love: My first love was working to promote the business of the one I loved with all of my heart, my Lord Jesus Christ.

While digging a basement and footing one day, the sky became very dark and just a little way distant you could see lightning and hear booming thunder. We had a large order of concrete ordered, and it was in-route. My help became concerned, knowing it was going to be hard to get the concrete poured in a downpour of rain. We had all of our tools out of the truck and ready to pour the concrete. Our laser was sitting on its tripod patiently spinning. My help had named the laser Toby, because when we purchased it a couple of years previously, it replaced a not so good helper that sometimes shot grade for us with an old fashioned transit building level whom they had named Toby.

Steve came over where I was running the backhoe, finishing up the last bit of digging. Steve always addressed me as boss. He said, "Boss, do you want me to put the tools in the truck?" I said, "Not yet." Steve said, "You don't want to get Toby wet. It cost a lot of money." I said, "Yes, Steve, it did cost a lot of money. I know that because I paid for it."

By now the rain had moved in, and it was raining on three sides of the property we were working on, but our lot was dry. I remembered a message I had preached. Following is the proclamation as written.

> And Elijah the Tishbite, who was of the inhabitants of Gilead, said unto Ahab, (a wicked king), As the Lord liveth, before whom I stand, there shall not be dew nor rain these years, but according to my word.
>
> I Kings 17:1

Here was a prophet of God looking a mean, nasty king in the eye and telling him, "It is not going to rain until I say so."

I don't consider myself a prophet, but I am a servant of God, out trying to make a living so we (Karen and I) can start another church or build another church building. So I looked at Steve and said, "It is not going to rain until we are finished. Don't worry about the tools." The concrete arrived, we poured probably 18 yards of concrete with thunder crashing and rain around the perimeter of the property. When the last bit of concrete was poured, we grabbed the tools and literally ran to the truck. When the tools were put away, the sky opened up and the rain came down in a mighty deluge.

I know this story may sound hard to believe, but after this particular day, Steve was a believer that I had control of the rain. At a later date, we had a similar incident, and the rain was coming. I had told the help, "Let's go ahead and get this poured." Steve was on the job again, along with a new helper. The new helper questioned me about us getting wet. Steve looked at him and said, "If the boss says it is not going to rain, you can rest assured, it's not going to rain until we are finished."

I only felt it necessary to speak in faith about the rain those couple of times. It was always when it would cause a major problem if we didn't get those jobs done in a timely manner. I thought if Elijah can do it, as a servant of God, I could expect God to do the same for me.

In my opinion, we have allowed ourselves to miss out on many miracles that God wanted to perform, but we were not willing to step out in faith and speak the word of faith. What could we accomplish for God if we actually took Him at His word and prayed the prayer of faith.

> And the Apostles said unto the Lord, Increase our faith. And the Lord said, If ye had faith as a grain of mustard seed ye might say unto this sycamine tree, Be thou plucked up by the root, and be thou planted in the sea; and it should obey you.
>
> Luke 17: 5-6

We say we believe the Word. I'm not sure we really understand how powerful this Scripture is. If we would take God at His word, there is no telling what kind of revival we would see break out. One person said, "It only takes one miracle to see a revival." Jesus said:

> Verily, verily, I say unto you, He that believeth on me, the works that I do shall he do also; and greater works that these shall he do; because I go to my Father.
>
> John 14:12

Did you get that? We can expect to do the works that Jesus did while He was on the earth, and He said we can even do greater works than those. Wow! Would you like to hear me say that backwards?? WOW!!

The stories I am telling are coming straight from my story book. If I come to one that I didn't see with my own eyes, I will tell you I didn't see it, but it came from a reliable source. It is my opinion that we need to hear about miracles that are happening. The Bible tells us that we go from faith to faith.

When we see a miracle, it tends to increase our belief that God can really perform miracles. It tends to cause our faith to soar. I believe we are fast moving into the last days, and if the church ever needed to have signs, wonders, and miracles this is the day. After seeing what God did for me in the last few months, I am a believer. I cannot explain to you the height God has raised my faith and trust.

There is another faith story that must be told. I mentioned this in my first book entitled *It's Not About Me, A life about Him*. Karen and I had felt the need to plant a new church in the Lawrenceburg—Aurora, Indiana, area. We had been toying with and praying about this sporadically for over ten years.

We would occasionally take a hundred mile drive and end up in that area. We would speak of the jobs that God called us to do as assignments. We had finished our last assignment and were just doing weekend ministry which allowed us some free time. It was a cold day in January when we got into the car to take a drive. It was as though the car was guiding itself as we left Brown County Indiana. We headed east and ultimately made the trip which we hadn't made for a while. We drove east on highway 50, passed through North Vernon, continued east through Holton, then through Versailles, and then on east through Dillsboro. The next area would be the Aurora and Lawrenceburg area.

Just a few miles before we got to Aurora, Karen pointed to the right side of the road to a beautiful facility on the edge of a commercial park and exclaimed, "There is our church building!" When I looked over there I saw a very expensive looking property with a "for sale" sign in front. Mind you, we were just driving over there to look around. As yet there were no plans of any kind, only the fact that we previously had said there needed to be a church in that area. Looking at, or buying buildings was certainly not on our agenda that day.

I basically told Karen if the Lord opened the windows of heaven this couldn't happen. We don't have a church. We don't even know if there will ever be a church in this area. My thoughts that day were that we just drive over there to eat lunch, and in a little while we would head back home. However, something in my spirit said it wouldn't hurt to take a look.

I made a U turn at the first crossover and went back to check out this property. I have a thing about buying properties, but at this time we didn't need a building. Who would we put in it if we had it? I am not known to be completely sane, but we did get out and look around this vacant property. Well, since we were there, we might as well get my Bible out of the car and go to the porch and pray about it and take some pictures.

You want to be careful what you pray. It might be a God thing, and you may just get what you pray for. We went on into Lawrenceburg and looked around. We had not, previously, given serious thought about planting a church there, so we hadn't even approached our North America Missions board about starting a new church. So we started the process to plant a new church in that area.

I talked to my sectional leader and told him what we intended to do. Then we got approval from our district board and North America Missions to start a church. We rented a not-so-nice property to have services. Our first service was scheduled for Friday, April 13, 2012. Notice, we started on Friday the 13th. We immediately started having people baptized and filled with the Holy Ghost. I am telling this story, in part, to show you that a positive word of faith, spoken by Karen, became a miracle, and eight months after we started a church we bought that facility. It had sold previously for $575,000, but we bought it for the paltry price of $200,000.

In one of the previous chapters I spoke about speaking positive words. Never allow yourself to get to the place where you begin to speak negative words. The more you speak negative, the more negative things you will have to say.

I am reminded of a story I once heard. Whether this story is true or not, I am not going to try and verify. Whether it is a true story or not, it can still be used to get the point across. It goes as follows:

There was a stately gentleman who had been very negative for a long time. One day he began to smell a foul odor. Everywhere he went that day, he kept complaining about the foul odor. He got in his car and complained that his car had a foul odor. He went into the local market, and the same smell was in the market.

Everywhere he went it was the same thing: "It stinks in here. My goodness, it sure stinks here." Later in the afternoon he saw a friend of his and immediately started complaining about the stench he had been smelling all day. His friend asked him, "What is that in your mustache?" He said, "I don't know." Upon examination, he found some Limburger cheese (a very foul smelling cheese) that had gotten stuck in his mustache when he had a snack earlier that day.

If everything in your life stinks, maybe something in your life needs to be changed. Maybe you should look in the mirror and see if you have something going on that makes you the way you are.

If all you can see is negative, you probably ought to change your negative glasses and put on some positive glasses. If you can't look at yourself and like yourself and speak positive about yourself, it is time to change yourself.

Finding God: My Journey Through Pancreatic Cancer

If, perhaps, you are a leader, or God forbid, even maybe a preacher, and if you are negative about yourself, how do you think others will look at you in a different light than you see yourself?

This next story I want to tell happened when I was still in business. I am telling this to show you that God cares about the things that you care about.

We installed a sewer line for a new house. The sewer and water lines are installed early in the building process, probably ninety days before the house is finished and the owner closes on his new house.

Karen and I had gone to Florida to see the kids and try to get a little bit of rest. While we were driving down the road, I received a phone call from the production manager of one of my builders. This particular man was extremely arrogant and thought he knew more than anyone else.

When I answered the phone, John was on the other end. He said, "We have a major situation going on with one of the sewer lines you installed, and it needs to be taken care of immediately or you are going to be sued."

We cut our vacation short and hurried home. I looked at our job sheet and saw that on this job the sewer line was under the new concrete driveway, and the production manager was cracking the whip to get it repaired. I knew that we had bedded the sewer line according to the Indianapolis code. Knowing this was going to be a high dollar repair, we were going to have to bring in a concrete sawing company to make a cut for us, then we would have to remove the concrete and haul it away, and then the driveway would need to be replaced after we repaired the sewer. When I laid down that night, I tossed and turned and all I could think about was the fact that we were going to end up with at least a $10,000 cost when this problem was fixed.

I was finally able to doze off. Sometime in the middle of the night, I had a dream. In my dream I saw the sewer line and where it left the yard area and went under the concrete driveway, and then had two forty-five degree elbows that made a ninety degree turn going straight down. In my dream I saw that one of the forty-five degree elbows had been smashed.

The next morning I told my help I knew where the problem was and it would be an easy fix. (Notice the positive conversation.) We took our equipment and dug a small hole beside the driveway and hand dug about two feet back under the driveway following the sewer pipe. We found the elbow that had been smashed. Within an hour's time we had the problem repaired.

We found out that the company that installed the basement wall had a problem with their wall and had to come back and repaired it. While working in there with a backhoe they had smashed our sewer with the stabilizer on their backhoe. I am so happy that God watches out for us and helps us when we are in need.

After we started the new church at Aurora, the Lord blessed us with the new property on US Highway 50. We had a large sign with the church name, Living Word Apostolic Church. Highway 50 was a four lane divided highway, and it carried a lot of traffic going in and out of Cincinnati.

Bob and Christine had retired from the Cincinnati area and had to pass Living Word regularly. When they lived in Cincinnati, they attended one of the local Apostolic churches. After retirement, they moved to Dillsboro, a small town about six miles down the road from Living Word.

Bob had a lot of health issues. He previously had many heart attacks, two or three strokes, and recently his kidneys had stopped working.

Finding God: My Journey Through Pancreatic Cancer

Due to the fact there was no Apostolic church in the area, they had been attending a local church of a different denomination but missed being in a Spirit filled church.

Due to his kidneys shutting down, they would pick Bob up three days a week and take him to Lawrenceburg for his dialysis treatment. One day Bob came home from his dialysis treatment, and when he came in the door he said to Christine, "You'll never believe what I saw today." Christine said, "Bob, what did you see?" She had no idea where Bob was going with this conversation. Bob said, "I saw a sign down the road by the motel. Would you believe that there is an Apostolic church just down the road."

Christine said, "We are going to have to go there." The next Sunday morning Bob and Christine were at church at Living Word and became regular attendees. At a later date Bob had another stroke. On Saturday evening Karen and I picked Christine up and took her to the hospital to visit Bob. He was in the critical care unit, and they were not expecting him to live through the night. His body was convulsing severely, and he did not recognize the fact that we were there to visit him.

He was secured to his bed so he wouldn't fall out and hurt himself. We prayed for him, and immediately Bob had a "but God" moment and became very calm.

We took Christine home and told her we would pick her up for church in the morning, and if Bob was still alive, we would take her to the hospital to visit with him. We left her that evening telling her that if Bob's condition worsened, give us a call and we will come and pick you up and take you to the hospital.

We picked her up for church Sunday morning. The title of my message that day was "But God." Following are some of the notes from that message:

> It is my intention today to speak a word of faith, and that someone will grasp hold of it and thereby be healed or receive the miracle you need.

> We must believe that when we pray, we unite ourselves with God. Then as we enter into His throne room, through prayer, He holds out His golden scepter toward us, allowing us to come into His presence.

My scriptural reference for the day was found in I Samuel 23:1-14.

> Then they told David, saying, behold the philistines fight against Keilah, and they rob the threshing floors. Therefore David inquired of the Lord saying, shall I go and smite these Philistines? And the Lord said unto David, go, and smite the Philistines, and save Keilah. And David's men said unto him, behold we be afraid here in Judah: how much more then if we come to Keilah against the armies of the Philistines? Then David inquired of the Lord yet again. And the Lord answered him and said, arise go down to Keilah; for I will deliver the Philistines into thine hand. So David and his men went to Keilah, and fought with the Philistines, and brought away their cattle, and smote them with a great slaughter. So David saved the inhabitants of Keilah. And it came to pass when Abiathar the son of Ahimelech fled to David in Keilah, that he came down with an ephod in his hand. And it was told Saul that

Finding God: My Journey Through Pancreatic Cancer

David was come to Keilah. And Saul said, God hath delivered him into mine hand; for he is shut in, by entering in to a city that hath gates and bars. And Saul called all the people together to war, to go down to Keilah, to besiege David and his men. And David knew that Saul secretly practiced mischief against him; and he said to Abiathar the priest, bring hither the ephod. Then said David, O Lord God of Israel, thy servant hath certainly heard that Saul seeketh to come to Keilah, to destroy the city for my sake. Will the men of Keilah deliver me up into his hand? Will Saul come down as thy servant hath heard? O Lord God of Israel, I beseech thee, tell thy servant. And the Lord God said, He will come down. Then David said, will the men of Keilah deliver me and my men into the hand of Saul? And the Lord said, They will deliver thee up. Then David and his men, which were about six hundred, arose and departed out of Keilah, and went withersoever they could go. And it was told Saul that David was escaped from Keilah; and he forbare to go forth. And David abode in the wilderness in strongholds, and remained in a mountain in the wilderness of Ziph. And Saul sought him every day, but God delivered him not into his hand.

I Samuel 23: 1-14

But Jesus beheld them, and said unto them, with men this is impossible, but with God all things are possible.

Matthew 19: 26

When Jesus shows up, all things are possible.

However, He does not always have to come to the place where you are, as you will see in the next Scriptures we will read. In these Scriptures, Jesus did a long distance healing.

> Now when he had ended all his sayings in the audience of the people. He entered into Capernaum. And a certain centurion's servant, who was dear unto him, was sick, and ready to die. And when he heard of Jesus, he sent unto him the elders of the Jews, beseeching him that he would come and heal his servant. And when they came to Jesus, they besought him instantly, saying, That he was worthy for whom he should do this. For he loveth our nation, and he hath built us a synagogue. Then Jesus went with them, And when he was not far from the house, the centurion sent friends to him, saying unto him, Lord, trouble not thyself: for I am not worthy that thou shouldest enter under my roof: Wherefore neither thought I myself worthy to come unto thee: but say in a word, and my servant shall be healed. For I also am a man set under authority, having under me soldiers, and I say unto one, Go, and he goeth; and to another, Come, and he cometh: and to my servant, Do this, and he doeth it. When Jesus heard these things, he marvelled at him, and turned him about, and said unto the people that followed him, I say unto you, I have not found so great faith, no not in Israel. And they that were sent, returning to the house, found the servant whole that had been sick.
>
> Luke 7: 1-10

We don't know anything about this man except that

he was sick, but when Jesus shows up, anything is possible!

I truly think it is about time we start figuring God into the equation, and therefore live a life without fear, knowing that God is in control, and He wants to fight our battles for us. Many times we get this attitude that God will not do anything for us because we don't deserve it.

If there was ever anyone who did not deserve Jesus doing anything for him, it was the man we read about in the Gospel of Luke, named Zacchaeus.

> And Jesus entered and passed through Jericho. And, behold, there was a man named Zacchaeus, which was chief among the publicans, and he was rich. And he sought to see Jesus who he was: and could not for the press, because he was little of stature. And he ran before, and climbed up into a sycamore tree to see him: for he was to pass that way. And when Jesus came to the place, he looked up, and saw him, and said unto him, Zacchaeus, make haste, and come down; for today I must abide at thy house. And he made haste, and came down, and received him joyfully. And when they saw it, they all murmured, saying, That he was gone to be guest with a man that is a sinner. And Zacchaeus stood, and said unto the Lord, the half of my goods I give to the poor; and if I have taken any thing from any man by false accusation, I restore him four-fold. And Jesus said unto him, This day is salvation come to this house, forasmuch as he

also is a son of Abraham. For the Son of man
is come to save that which was lost.

Luke 19: 1-10

Here is a man that, by no earthly means, would be
worthy for Jesus to do anything for him, much less
come into his house. But God does not look at the
fact of whether or not we are deserving, but when He
sees a heart that is hungry and seeking for Him, he
makes himself available. As it said in verse 10, "He
came to seek and save the lost."

You may say, "I've been too bad, I'm not worthy,
God's not interested in me." If you only knew how
God feels about you, it would blow your mind.

Paul told Timothy: "This is a faithful saying, and
worthy of all acceptation, that Christ Jesus came into
the world to save sinners; of whom I am chief" (I
Timothy 1:15). I am not saying God will not move
for a person who does not have a right relationship
with Him, but it is easier for that person to petition
God for their needs if they have a good relationship
with Him.

After preaching the message, "But God," we took Christine to the
hospital to check on Bob. We wondered what we would see when
we got there because of the critical condition he was in the previous
evening as he convulsed and his body shook so terribly. But when
we entered the critical care unit and turned to go down the corridor
to his room, he heard footsteps in the hallway and was leaning out
of his hospital bed looking to see who was coming. During the
night, after we had prayed for him, his critical condition made a U
turn, and in one night his condition moved from not going to make

it through the night to "you're fine, and you can go home today." He went home and didn't have any negative side-affects from this serious stroke. There was no hope eighteen hours earlier, but God miraculously changed no hope into get ready to go home.

More Miracles

My phone rang. On the other end was our son, Nick, who was the pastor of the first church we had started. He said, "We have an emergency going on here." Scott was knocked out and had no pulse, and his lips had turned blue. I had just come in from work and was standing at the sink, shaving. I began shouting, "No! No! I refuse this in Jesus Name." I picked up my phone and called Karen and Leah, Scott's wife, who were riding in the car together. I later heard that when I called them they began to pray the same prayer I had prayed, "No! No! I refuse this, in Jesus Name."

Scott was playing basketball at the school where he had graduated. This was a game played between the alumni and the senior varsity team. As he was dribbling the ball down the floor, he was knocked down, and his head hit the floor. This was a school that openly taught against speaking with tongues. Nick ran down from the bleachers, onto the basketball floor, and laid hands on him, praying for him and began speaking in tongues. As Nick was praying, the local EMT team arrived with an ambulance. Paul Burpo, one of the EMT's, a large man, bent over to work on Scott, hopefully to revive him and get him breathing again. When Paul bent over him, the Lord did what only He could do, and Scott began breathing again and literally threw Paul off.

Since he had all of the symptoms of death, they decided he needed to go to the hospital and be checked out. He said, "I am not going to the hospital, I am going to my sister's birthday party." Satan said , "Death come on, but God said, "It is not time to die," and He rebuked death and said, "It is time to live."

Upon arriving at the hospital, the doctors asked what symptoms he had when he was knocked out. When the doctor heard that he had stopped breathing, his lips turned blue, and he had a seizure, he said, "According to what you are telling me, he should not be responding the way he is to all of the tests I have given him. We need to keep him over night to make sure he is alright." Scott said, "I am not staying here in the hospital, I am going to my sister's birthday party." Guess what he did? He went to Chris' birthday party and had no other issues. I am so happy that when we need God, He is an on time God.

Scott's wife, Leah, at thirty four years of age, was having a lot of issues with her health and eventually decided it was time to see a doctor. Upon examination, it was determined that she had stage three colorectal cancer.

She submitted to chemotherapy treatment and then had surgery. After having numerous examinations during the next six years, each year she has been given a cancer free diagnosis. After surgery she continued doing chemotherapy with its many side effects. Because of the side effects, her chemotherapy treatments were canceled. After her original diagnosis of stage three, we feel that God has, indeed, done a great work in her life, and we are so thankful that God is still in control. At her last doctor visit the doctor said, "We typically do not see results like this after having your original diagnosis."

When pastoring at Beanblossom, a young couple, Jenny and Mike, came to church and received the Holy Ghost. Mike decided that he just didn't want to live for God, and at around the same time decided he was going to leave Jenny. In this same time period they were expecting their first child.

Mike left Jenny and the new baby, Danielle, in some pretty severe living conditions. Jenny was a new convert, and not wanting all of her bad circumstances to kill her spiritually, we helped her along to keep her encouraged and serving the Lord. We helped her move into one of our rental apartments.

As if that wasn't enough, with all of the other hurtful circumstances, her baby, Danielle, began having health issues. After examination, it was determined that Danielle had heart problems. The doctors not only said she had heart problems but she had serious heart problems, so serious that she was going to need a heart transplant.

Jenny took her to the hospital for more testing and to try and schedule her for whatever treatment they determined she would need. Karen and I went to be with Jenny while they were running the different tests on her baby. After quite a while the doctors had not, as yet, come out to give her the results of the test. As the time slowly passed, we waited with Jenny, not wanting her to be alone when the doctors determined what they needed to do about treating Danielle's heart condition. We had gone down to the hospital cafeteria to get a bite to eat and also make sure Jenny had money to buy her lunch. It became apparent that we would need to leave before the doctors came back with their diagnosis.

We stood up to leave and I said, "We need to pray before we go." We stood there in a little circle, holding hands and praying, believing that somehow God was going to fix this problem.

I encouraged Jenny to not be surprised when the doctor tells you, "We can't find anything wrong with her heart." We left and went to our appointment. Sometime later we received a phone call. Jenny said, "I have the results from all of the testing." I asked, "What did they say?" She said, "The doctor said, '"We can't find anything wrong with her heart.'" These were the exact words that I had left her with.

The Lord sent Jenny a good husband, a man that not only loved her but also became a dad to Danielle. Because of Jenny's commitment to God and the church, God restored everything that she had lost but much more. The Bible says, "Now unto him that is able to do exceeding abundantly above all that we ask or think, according to the power that worketh in us" (Ephesians 3:20).

Jenny has been so faithful to God, and He has not only blessed her with what she had lost, but He restored abundantly above and more than she could even believe. Jenney's husband, Steve, is a great man and serves God with all of his heart. They live in a new house, drive a new car, never miss a church service, and love the Lord with all their hearts. They are very financially stable and are never stingy with God or their fellow man.

While pastoring at Beanblossom, one morning I woke up at 4:00 and was extremely ill. I finally got out of bed at 6:00. We had a young man from the church that was having his tonsils removed that day, and being his pastor, I felt like I should be there to give him and his family some moral support, so Karen and I went to Bloomington to be there for them.

When we left the hospital I was extremely sick, so Karen drove us home. Now, I was so sick that I had her stop beside the road a couple of times so I could throw up. We finally got home around 11:30 am. Because I was extremely sick, I immediately went to bed. One minute I would have cold chills, and the next minute I was burning up with a fever. That continued all afternoon, along with numerous trips to the bathroom.

As the day passed, the sickness got even more severe. Oh my, this is Wednesday, I thought. We have church tonight, and I have a visiting minister coming to preach. Oh well, I guess Karen and Nick II can handle it, but I want to go to church, and I was still having the hot flashes and cold chills going on.

I had gotten up for a few minutes and immediately went back to bed. There was no way I was going to make it to church without a miracle. I didn't think I could even get out of bed, let alone go to church. You know when you're the pastor you go to church even if you are sick, as long as your sickness is not contagious. Looks like this old boy won't be going to church, I thought. I could hardly stand up, let alone drive a car.

As I lay in bed I heard our son Scott downstairs singing. The words to the song he was singing said, "I know satan and his imps will come to torment me. When I invoke the name of Jesus every demon has to flee."

About that time Karen came into the bedroom and asked if I was going to church. I said, "That would be impossible without a miracle." About that time I heard Scott coming upstairs, and I called for him to come into the bedroom and pray for me. At that time he had never yet voiced the fact that he felt a call from God to enter the ministry, and to my knowledge, had never prayed for a sick person. I think he was shocked, but he went and got mom to help him pray. It was 4:50 in the afternoon when they prayed. I felt God's presence and began to pray in the Spirit. Then I remembered that a book I had read talked about drug addicts coming off of drugs with no symptoms of withdrawal as long as they kept praying in the Spirit. I was feeling God's Spirit in a very strong way, and He began to speak to me something I had read in Bishop Kenneth Haney's book: *The Anointed Ones.*[5] It was the part that expressed, "Faith without works is dead." I said to myself, I am going to get up and get ready for church. I got up, took a shower, polished my shoes, got dressed for church, and was at the church one hour before service started, completely healed and praising God. I will tell you without reservation that God still does what He said He would do. When my faith became action, and I got out of bed, God healed me. Hallelujah!!!!

The Process

While preaching for Pastor Ron Cox in Brownstown, Indiana, on May 30, 2019, I was preaching a message that I titled "The Process." The message is as follows:

> The Scripture I am using is found in Exodus 2:23-25 and reads: "And it came to pass in the process of time, that the king of Egypt died: and the children of Israel sighed by reason of the bondage, and they cried, and their cry came up unto God by reason of the bondage. And God heard their groaning, and God remembered his covenant with Abraham, and with Isaac, and with Jacob. And God looked upon the children of Israel, and God had respect unto them."

> Somehow I want to encourage someone to believe that it really is possible to have the personal relationship with God that you have always wanted and have been striving for. It is not my intention to try and impress anyone. My main goal is to help someone move from the spiritual level you are on today and take you up to the next level spiritually. If I would strive to impress, it would be to impress God by helping someone in their spiritual process to find God in a special way.

> Being saved and staying saved is a work in progress. It starts with being born again of water (being baptized in Jesus Name according to the book of Acts). Next is to receive the Holy Ghost (Holy Spirit) evidenced by speaking with tongues and continuing by living a holy life separated from the world.

Finding God: My Journey Through Pancreatic Cancer

Recently, when I was praying very intensely, I told God, "I am always trying to attain a certain level—a certain place in God but never quite attaining the goal I am aiming for. It is always just beyond my reach." I have come to the conclusion that God doesn't want us to totally attain our spiritual aspirations. He wants us to always need Him, otherwise, we would think that we have arrived and have no need for him. Oh, God, if only I could know you!!!!

> That I may know him, and the power of his resurrection, and the fellowship of his suffering, being made conformable unto his death. If by any means I might attain unto the resurrection of the dead. Not as though I had already attained, either were already perfect: but I follow after, if that I may apprehend that for which I am apprehended of Jesus Christ. Brethren, I count not myself to have apprehended: but this one thing I do, forgetting those things which are behind, and reaching forth unto those things which are before, I press toward the mark for the prize of the high calling of God in Christ Jesus.
>
> Philippians 3: 10–14

I believe that few things in life just happen and that many of the things which do happen are just part of God's process in order to bring us into total subjection of His will. I can tell you from experience, when issues too big for me to handle come along, they bring me closer to Jesus.

We all want God's will for our lives but think we have the ability in our own selves to reach that goal. My ultimate goal is to hear Him say, "WELL DONE."

I have found out in life and business there are sometimes different ways to reach a goal. That may be true in the natural, but in the spiritual realm there is only one way, and that is God's way. The men that worked for me sometimes did certain things differently than I was used to doing them, and I found out that sometimes their way of doing a certain thing could arrive at the same goal as my way of doing it. However, in spiritual things, there is only one way—God's way.

Many times we pray, God, I want to do your will, but when God gives direction—maybe with a still small voice—we never totally submit to His leading. The process goes on. When we fail to adapt to God's will, the spiritual process applies the brakes and the process goes on hold until we are ready to really submit to God. Then we just continue to plod along the same old way we have always gone until God applies the pressure again by the same means or possibly a different means.

We sometimes just keep plodding along with no change, thinking God is going to adapt to our way of thinking and desires. Sorry, there are not two or three ways with God. It's His way or the highway. As we journey along, God patiently tries to guide us toward the goals He has designed for us, and many times we just keep going down the same old path. God really tries to direct, and we casually drift along off the path

He has designed for us.

Being saved and staying saved is a work in progress. We have not arrived until that great day when we step across the threshold of heaven. Oh, what a wonderful day that will be! There will be some pain and discomfort in the shaping process, but heaven will be worth all of the discomfort. Our journey will not be a bed of roses. Sometimes there will be a thorn. We may have good ideas, but if they are not what God has designed for us, they just won't work.

Since our spiritual lives are a work in progress, you can't rush the process. Nature lets us know that it takes time for fruit to mature. Just as it takes time for fruit to mature, it also takes time for our spiritual house to be built. As we progress in the process, we are all on different levels. It's like being in school. There are different grades. God does not intend for us to remain in the first grade at ten years of age. It is His intentions that we keep moving forward and passing the test to move up to the next grade. In order to pass from one grade to the next, you are going to have to work at it.

God will allow you to stay in the same spiritual grade as long as it takes for you to graduate. The Scripture says, "Strive to enter in at the strait gate; for many, I say unto you, will seek to enter in, and shall not be able" (Luke 13:24).

The word strive means:

1. To contend with adversaries (fight).

2. To struggle with difficulties.
3. To endeavor with strenuous zeal.

All of the above explanations (contend, struggle, endeavor, and strenuous) speak of something that takes effort. Anything worth doing or having is worth working for. I can speak from experience and say that the thing which will bring you the greatest joy and satisfaction in life is when you submit to the Master Shepherd and allow Him to direct your life. Stop trying to direct your own life. Let go and let God have your reins.

You may ask, "What will this Christ journey cost me?" It will only cost you everything, nothing less. The old hymn by Audrey Mieir says:[6]

> All He wants is you, no one else will do,
> Not just a part, He wants all of your heart,
> All He wants is all of you,
> All he wants is you.

Things in life are constantly changing. Jesus never changes; still, all He wants is you.

At the end of the service I felt impressed to have an old fashioned prayer line. I asked all the people to come through the line. When they came through we prayed for them and then they joined those who were praying at the end of the line.

There was one man in particular that was having a conversation with himself. He said, "I don't even know if I believe in prayer lines, but what do I have to lose?" So Brother Freed came through the line to be prayed for. I received a phone call from his pastor on Wednesday, and he said that I know you didn't know this, but Brother Freed had lost his voice, and the doctor told him he may never be able to speak audibly with his voice again, but by Wednesday his voice had returned. He was very excited when his neighbors noticed that his voice had returned, and he was able to tell them it returned after being prayed for in the prayer line at church. His testimony was, "The Lord has healed my voice, and now I can speak above a whisper." What a great God we serve.

Thank God there is nothing impossible for the King of kings and the Lord of lords. I am reminded of an old chorus titled *Only Believe*.[7] It is a simple little chorus and goes as follows:

> Only believe, only believe;
> All things are possible, only believe;
> Only believe, only believe;
> All things are possible, only believe.

What a simple little chorus but packed full to the brim with faith. As I have heard many choruses and songs through the years, I often wonder what was going on in the life of the people who wrote them? What kinds of situations were they facing? Were they having health issues? Were they broken hearted because one of their children strayed from God? Were they facing a serious sickness, with no way of knowing what the end result would be? Had they lost a spouse through death? Were they facing divorce after being married for twenty years?

Mom

After dad passed away, mom was content to live alone. What a change! They had literally been together almost every day for many years and were rarely separated. She really never complained about being lonesome, although we knew that she had to be lonely.

Some years after dad's passing, mom also passed away. As we were cleaning out her apartment, we found a notebook in which she had apparently written at times when she was probably lonely or discouraged. I found one section that was dated three years after dad's passing. It is as follows. I am writing her thoughts as she had written them, without editing or giving any credit or references to quotes.[8]

Yes He understands, All His ways are best
Hear He calls to you, Come to me and rest
Leave the unknown future, In the Master's hands
Whether sad or joyful, Jesus understands.

Love not the world, neither the things that are in the world, If any man love the world, the love of the Father is not in him.

I have too much invested in this salvation to ever think about turning back. From the time I first started working (I made 25 cents an hour.) a part time job in a butcher shop, I paid tithes on that, and it also provided bus or street car fare to go to church. As far as I know, I have paid tithes on everything we have ever made, plus lots of offerings.

One time when we were in financial trouble, the Lord reminded me that we have always paid our tithes, and the bank of heaven never goes broke and when you have money invested in a bank that you draw interest on your account. I guess, probably, I have thousands of dollars credited to my account, and I don't want to do anything stupid and lose my inheritance. We have never had an abundance of earthly things, but we have always had our needs supplied. We have always had food and raiment, a place to live, and clothing to wear.

As of October 25, 1997 I will have sixty-one years invested in this way (the Lord's way), and I have no intention of losing out now.

But the Lord is so wonderful—if anyone comes in and is filled with the Holy Ghost the day before the coming of the Lord, he will be caught up and escape all the things that are coming on this world.

I believe the Lord requires faithfulness, that we should be in the house of God every time the doors are open—that we have no excuse. If we are sick the Bible says to call for the elders of the church, and the prayer of faith shall save the sick, and the Lord will raise him up.

If we are faithful to the Lord, He will also be faithful to us. When our children were very young, Lee was in the hospital several times—once with ruptured appendix, then with cavernous sinus thrombosis, caused from a boil on his nose—then later for several surgeries, but the Lord always provided for us during these times of trouble. It is 12:15 AM, time to go to bed.

Oh the unsearchable riches of God, wealth that can never be told. Oh the unsearchable riches of God, precious more precious than gold.

No weapon that is formed against you shall prosper (Isaiah 54).

Nick Seniour

In the presence of the Lord there is fulness of joy.

My God shall supply all your needs according to His riches in glory.

I've seen the lightning flashing, I've heard the thunder roll
I've felt sins breakers dashing, Truing to conquer my soul,
I've heard the voice of my Savior, telling me still to fight on,
He promised never to leave me, never to leave me alone.

Thy word is a lamp unto my feet and a light unto my pathway.

It reaches to the highest mountain
It flows to the lowest valley
The blood that gives me strength from day to day
Will never lose its power.
What can wash away my sin? Nothing but the blood of Jesus,
What can make me whole again, nothing but the blood of Jesus,
Oh precious is the flow, That makes me white as snow,
No other fount I know, Nothing but the blood of Jesus.

What will it be when we get over yonder,
And join the throng around the glassy sea,
To greet our loved ones and crown Christ forever,
Oh this is just what heaven means to me.

Finding God: My Journey Through Pancreatic Cancer

Just lift me up and let me stand,
By faith on heaven's stable land,
A higher plain than I have found,
Lord plant my feet on higher ground.

Oh Lord prepare me, to be a sanctuary,
Pure and holy, tried and true,
And with thanksgiving, I'll be a living,
Sanctuary for you.
God is still on the throne, and he never forsaketh his own,
Though trials may press us, and burdens distress us,
He never will leave us alone.
God is still on the throne, and he will remember his own,
His promise is true, he will not forget you, God is still on the throne.

Oh just think how in death you would feel,
With the light growing dim in your soul,
Oh how lonely t'would be, oh how still,
If the light has gone out in your soul.

II Corinthians 12:9 And he said unto me, my grace is sufficient for thee: for my strength is made perfect in weakness. Most gladly therefore will I rather glory in my infirmities, that the power of Christ may rest upon me.

Isaiah 40:31 But they that wait upon the Lord Shall renew their strength: they shall mount up with wings as eagles: they shall run, and not be weary, and they shall walk and not faint. (Teach me Lord, teach me Lord to wait.)

Nick Seniour

He was wounded for our transgressions,
He was bruised for our iniquities,
Surely he bore our sorrows,
 And by his stripes we are healed.

I'm longing for Jesus to come back,
I long for Jesus Christ my Lord
To come and take me to my home beyond the sky,
Up there where angels shout and sing.

Sweep over my soul, sweep over my soul,
Sweet Spirit sweep over my soul,
My joy is complete, when I kneel at his feet,
Sweet Spirit sweep over my soul.

Let me look past the curtain of sorrow and tears
Let me view that sunny bright clime,
Just to strengthen my faith and banish all fears,
Let me look past the curtain of time.

He knew just what I needed most, yes he did, yes he
did,
When he baptized me with the Holy Ghost, yes he
did, yes he did.
You can tell the world about this, you can tell the
nations we're blessed,
Tell them what Jesus has done, tell them that the
comforter has come
And he brought joy, great joy to my soul.

So when I'm bent beneath some load of care,
Just remind me that I'm almost there, Just remind me
that I'm nearing home.

Finding God: My Journey Through Pancreatic Cancer

> My heart can sing when I pause to remember,
> A heartache here is but a stepping stone,
> Along the trail that's winding always upward,
> This troubled world is not my final home.
>
> But until then, my heart will go on singing,
> Until then with joy I'll carry on,
> Until the day my eyes behold that city,
> Until the day, God calls me home.

My precious mother wrote these thoughts, songs, and Scriptures after the passing of my dad in 1994. They speak of a lady who was lonely, but she was very strong in spirit. What made her so strong in spirit? Her being strong in spirit was simply because of somewhere near a sixty-five year relationship with Jesus Christ, the One who had sustained her when her mother and father had divorced when she was just a young girl.

This same Jesus had kept her through the years when Lee boy was away from God and would come home drunk. That same Jesus had taken care of her during the struggles she had in her early years of marriage, and it was her relationship with God and her constant prayer that brought Lee boy back to God and started the progression of ministry in the Seniour family.

It is because of Janet Louise Seniour and W. Lee Seniour that as a young boy following their lead that God put in my heart a desire to serve and be pleasing to God. I am so thankful that I was called of God, and I chose to commit my life, number one, to making disciples for Christ, instead of making money.

As I sit here at my computer I find myself quoting one of mom's quotes. Oh the unsearchable riches of God, Wealth that can never be told, Oh the unsearchable riches of God, precious, more precious than gold.[9]

What an amazing life when you really find God. How amazing to get past all the religiosity and spiritual fluff and come face to face with The Only Living God, manifest in flesh. I thank God that I know Him personally. Would you pardon me for a minute as I step away from my computer for a few minutes so I can stand to my feet and worship my King? Hallelujah!!!!

Thank God for my heritage. Thank God that my mom and dad set the stage for me to experience God for myself. Thank God for all of the health issues I have had this year. After having served the Lord for many years, and when I felt like God was nowhere near and I began to search for Him anew, He came to me. I found God in a fuller measure!

I found, once again, that when you search for Him, He can be found. You may ask me, "What in the world are you talking about?" I can only tell you that what I feel is joy unspeakable and full of glory. He is more than all this world to me.

Yes, I have had the Holy Spirit for many years. Yes, I have spoken in other tongues. Yes, I have served God to the best of my ability, and yes, what you are feeling right now is what I am talking about. It is time to receive everything God has for you. God desires that you live in the realm of the Spirit where He can communicate with you.

There is more to God that hearing about Him. There is more to God than just confessing Him with your mouth. There is more to God than saying, "I believe." It is possible to have a personal relationship with the creator of the universe. It is possible to hear Him speak to you.

Searching

You may try to push aside what you are feeling right now. Why did you buy this book? If you weren't searching for more of God, why would you want to find Him? I wanted to find Him, not because He was lost, but because at that moment I was not able to even feel His presence. I was so overwhelmed with all of my health issues and life in general that, at that moment, I felt forsaken and hopeless. I was used to having a relationship with God, but at that moment I would have been thankful for a slight spiritual breeze. But because of my search for Him, He came to me in an even more powerful way than ever before.

I realize I am speaking to some people who desire to have a fuller relationship with God. After searching for a little while, you have come to the conclusion that your spiritual status today will be your status from now on. I want to encourage you to keep searching. God has not forsaken you, He is just giving you time to get real hungry. "Blessed are they which do hunger and thirst after righteousness: for they shall be filled" (Matthew 5:6).

The above Scripture speaks of being hungry and thirsty. For someone to be hungry and thirsty, this suggests that they have been lacking food and water for a period of time. So you searched for that greater relationship with God and, so far, it doesn't seem as though it is going to happen. Maybe you have become discouraged and have settled for a little touch from God or just knowing about God. When there is a hunger and thirst, you may be able to pacify your hunger and thirst with an occasional touch of God's Spirit, but when you have experienced that special touch one time, it will cause you to keep hungering again and again. Status quo will never satisfy after you have pushed through and had that special touch.

I stated, earlier that one day I was praying very intensely and told God, "I am always trying to attain a certain level—a certain place in God—but never quite reaching the goal I am striving for. It is always just beyond my spiritual reach." I have come to the conclusion that

Nick Seniour

God doesn't want us to completely reach that goal we are searching for and totally fulfill our aspirations. He will move us forward just a little bit but never totally attain the level we are longing for. He wants us to always need Him; otherwise, we would think that we have arrived and have no need for Him.

Once you get that special drink from the spiritual well, there will always be a desire for another drink. During this process of seeking to find God, you cannot allow yourself to become discouraged and stop the process of seeking. That is where faith enters the picture. Hebrews tells us that without faith it is impossible to please God. "But without faith it is impossible to please him: for he that cometh to God must believe that he is, and that he is a rewarder of them that diligently seek him" (Hebrews 11:6).

There is something about God that I believe He desires us to continually need Him. I need Him so much and so often that sometimes I get embarrassed. God, am I such a wimp that I am not able to order my own life, even my very own footsteps? I have to admit, I REALLY DO NEED HIM.

I have found that when we seek first the kingdom of God and His righteousness that all of our natural needs just kind of take care of their selves (Matthew 6:33). I believe that when we live our lives being available to Him, He, then, becomes available to us.

You may feel the way I did before I finally submitted to His will for my life. I was fearful what it may require of me if I were to totally submit to His cause. I finally took the leap and left the results to Him. What I found out was that when He is in the driver's seat, the things that looked so impossible to my human eyes previously, now became doable because of my trust being in God's direction and His ability to handle the steering wheel of my life. I began to see impossibilities become possibilities (Mark 9:23).

Finding God: My Journey Through Pancreatic Cancer

The Apostle Peter

The apostle Peter found out that with God all things are possible when he literally stepped out of the boat and went walking to Jesus on the water. We all know it is impossible for us to walk on the water. I wonder what was it in Peter that he would, even for a fleeting moment, desire to walk on the water. What was his purpose for wanting to walk on water?

Was it because he had never seen it done before? Was he on an ego trip? Did he want to go down in history as one who walked on water? If that was the case, he sure flunked out on that one. Was he just testing Jesus to see if He would help him? We may never know the reason Peter wanted to walk on the water, but one thing we do know is that Peter did walk on water. You may point an accusing finger at him, with all kinds of negative things to say about him, but until you do what he did, maybe you might just want to retract that pointed finger until you do what he did. I do know he did a lot of things I have never been able to accomplish. He has been labeled with a lot of different names that if you didn't know his whole story you might wonder what kind of guy he was. Peter's life was a mixture of strange things. He could go from a life of real faith to the lowest depths of doubt.

We first hear of Peter in the 4th chapter of Matthew.

> And Jesus, walking by the sea of Galilee, saw two brethren, Simon called Peter, and Andrew his brother, casting a net into the sea: for they were fishers. And he saith unto them, Follow me, and I will make you fishers of men. And they straightway (immediately), left their nets (they just got up out of the boat, leaving their nets and fishing equipment), and followed him.
>
> Matthew 4:18-20

Nick Seniour

Here we have two men who, upon being invited by Jesus to join His team, were so impressed by Him that they would just leave their livelihood and equipment and jump out of the boat to go help Jesus fish for men. What was it about Jesus that would cause two grown men to make this, what some would call a rash or hasty decision? With what information we have available to us, it was only one verse earlier that Jesus began His ministry after being tempted by the devil.

Jesus was able to withstand all of the devil's temptation because he had been led of the Spirit into the wilderness. He then endured the temptation of the devil. He had also fasted forty days and forty nights. After having heard the voice of the Lord (finding God), I can only assure you that there is something about having heard the voice of the Lord that demands attention!

In my case I heard the Lord speak through a dream, and it was so powerful—so authoritative—that it demanded immediate attention. It was so real that I sat up in bed and responded. I not only sat up and responded, but I responded by speaking back to the messenger by saying, "That's mine, I am claiming it," while pointing my finger at the messenger. Then when Karen got out of bed, I spoke in faith to her saying, "It's over," and two days later it was indeed over. The five weeks of this problem with no natural or medical possibility of being over, ended two days after me finding God.

Now, six months later, I am still emotionally out of control simply because the one true living God, the Creator and Ruler of this great universe, chose to speak peace and healing into my life. What a great and powerful God we serve!

Whatever it was that caused Peter to walk away from the fishing boat and his career also created faith and great power in his life: so much power that we find him, along with John, walking into the temple at the daily prayer time. There sitting at the gate was a man who had been lame since the day he was born. He was begging for a few coins to help him with his meager existence. We find this familiar story in the Book of Acts:

> Now Peter and John went up together into the temple at the hour of prayer, being the ninth hour. And a certain man lame from his mother's womb was carried, whom they laid daily at the gate of the temple which is called Beautiful, to ask alms of them that entered into the temple; Who seeing Peter and John about to go into the temple asked an alms. And Peter, fastening his eyes upon him with John, said Look on us. And he gave heed unto them, expecting to receive something of them. Then Peter said, silver and gold have I none, but such as I have give I thee: in the name of Jesus Christ of Nazareth rise up and walk. And he took him by the right hand, and lifted him up: and immediately his feet and ankle bones received strength. And he leaping up stood, and walked, and entered with them into the temple, walking and leaping, and praising God. And all of the people saw him walking and praising God. And they knew that It was he which sat for alms at the Beautiful gate of the temple: and they were filled with wonder and amazement at that which had happened unto him.
>
> Acts 3:1–10.

Some people only remember Peter as being the one who denied Christ. We read in Matthew 26 at the Passover supper that Jesus broke the bread and gave it to His disciples and told them to eat of it, explaining that the bread was His body. Then he took the cup, gave thanks, and gave it to them, telling them to drink all of it.

Then He explained, "This is the blood of the new testament, which is shed for many for the remission of sins." They then sang a hymn and went out to the mount of Olives. Jesus then told them, "All ye shall be offended because of me this night: for it is written, I will smite the shepherd, and the sheep of the flock shall be scattered abroad. But after I am risen again I will go before you into Galilee."

Peter speaks up and says, "Though all men shall be offended because of you, yet I will never be offended." Jesus spoke to him and said, "This very night before a single rooster crows, you will deny and disown Me three times." Peter responded, "Even if I have to die with you, I will never deny or disown you." Then they all went to a place called Gethsemane where Jesus tells his disciples to "Sit here while I go a little farther and pray." Jesus then took Peter and the two sons of Zebedee and began to be sorrowful and very heavy in spirit.

He then tells them that His soul is very sorrowful, even unto death, you stay here and watch with me. And he went a little farther and fell on his face and prayed, saying, "O my Father, if it be possible let this cup pass from me: nevertheless not as I will but as thou will."

He came back to His disciples and found them sleeping, gave them a little reprimand, and went back and prayed again. After praying three times that the cup may be taken from Him, Judas came with a great company and gave Jesus the Judas kiss, and they took Jesus away.

The Bible says that all the disciples forsook Him and ran away. Oh, what fear gripped them! I can just see them running, breathing hard, panting, then slowing down and looking over their shoulder to see if anyone was following. Peter, the one who had so vehemently told Jesus that, "Though all men shall be offended because of you, I will never be offended!" followed Jesus, but he stayed far enough back to not be recognized as one being with Jesus. The Scripture says he

Finding God: My Journey Through Pancreatic Cancer

followed Jesus but from afar.

We know that his conscience had to be working overtime. Peter, you know you told Jesus that if everyone forsook him, you wouldn't. The next time we hear about Peter, he is sitting by the palace, and a young lady approaches him and says, "You were with Jesus of Galilee." He responded by saying, "I don't know what you are talking about." He goes out to the porch, and another young lady said, "This fellow was also with Jesus of Nazareth." He denied again with an oath and said, "I do not know the man." A little while later someone else said to Peter, "Surely you are one of them, for your speech clearly betrays you." Then he began to curse and swear, saying, "I don't know that man." And immediately the rooster began to crow. And Peter remembered the words of Jesus when he had said, before the rooster crows, you will deny me three times. And he went out and wept bitterly.

I can only imagine the feeling, knowing that he had done what he had so boldly proclaimed he wouldn't do. His thoughts? I remember when He came by my fishing boat and I just jumped out of the boat and followed Him. I have been with Him, in His inner circle. I was the one Jesus had given the keys to the Kingdom. I was his right hand man, and I just cursed and said I didn't even know Him.

You talk about feeling bad: we will probably never know Peter's feelings at that moment, but after the crucifixion, Peter was used mightily by God when he preached the powerful sermon on the day of Pentecost.

Let's try to wrap this up. We first hear about Peter when he was in the fishing boat and Jesus called him to come and help him fish for men. We don't know what caused Peter to just jump up and follow Jesus. I have given this much thought and have come to the conclusion that the only reason Peter would just drop everything and follow Jesus was there was something about Jesus that demanded his attention. Then it was the words out of Jesus' mouth that would cause him to follow Jesus.

There is such a power displayed when you hear the Word of the Lord. I know that after my quest to find God, and then hearing from Him, my life has never been the same. I can't even imagine what it will be like when we see Him face to face.

David said in the Psalms: "One thing have I desired of the Lord, that will I seek after; that I may dwell in the house of the Lord all the days of my life, to behold the beauty of the Lord, and to inquire in his temple" (Psalms 27:4).

Although Peter was impulsive by nature and just jumped out of the boat and went with Jesus and then denied Him, we still find Him preaching a powerful message on the day of Pentecost. What was it that made such a change in Peter's life?

The thing that changed Peter's life happened in the Book of Acts when they were all gathered in an upper room in Jerusalem. They were instructed to wait in an upper room for the promise of the Father, and that promise was that they would be filled with the Holy Ghost. In Acts 1:8 they were given the promise that when they received the Holy Ghost they would also receive power.

Some More Miracles

In 1984 my father in-law, Harry Dawson, was diagnosed as having lung cancer. When the surgeon opened him up for surgery, he took a look and just sewed him back up. He told the family there was no use in trying to take this cancer out because it was far too advanced to even hope for a cure. The surgeon said his life expectancy would be about three months. Evidently, God didn't see eye to eye with the surgeon, because Harry lived another thirteen and a half years and eventually passed away with colon cancer.

I am very thankful for the doctors and those in the medical field. They work tirelessly and to the best of their ability to find a problem and make a diagnosis. It is an amazing thing to have equipment that can scan your body and tell if you have a tumor, or cancer, or many other things going on. At least it gives you something to worry about. Then they treat these problems with the latest medicines and technology, hoping for the best results, but I am so glad that the final outcome rests in the hands of God. God says, "It's not over until I say so." When it is all said and done, our great-big, wonderful, mighty, powerful, and all knowing God has the last word. Without a doubt, He is my Savior, Keeper, and Healer, and I place my trust in HIM.

Thanks to all of the doctors that helped me in my health journey in 2020. Thanks to Doctor Ali Dohan for being alert with a speedy recognition of the problem, and to Doctor Troiano for his immediate help with the procedure to open my bile duct and get a diagnosis of the problem. Then a great big thank you to my oncologist, Doctor Raghavendra, and her treatment program, and also Doctor House who performed the Whipple surgery. Ultimately, my heart felt thank you to Jesus Christ Who has the final outcome in his great, big hands. I don't know what I would do without having Him to control all aspects of my life.

On a little different line of thought, we had a very dear family friend Named Earl Raley. Earl was a member of the Merchant Marines and had been on active duty. I can't remember which conflict he was involved in, but he was now discharged and back home again. When he got home, he started a very profitable business, that of building new houses. He and Ann, his wife, had no children, so they adopted a baby boy. Life was moving along at a nice pace, business was good, and his son, Danny, was growing up. Life couldn't have gotten much better. As is many times the case, in this time of prosperity, another war had broken out, and Uncle Sam decided that they needed Earl to come back into service. His booming business had to be shut down, and once again, he had to leave Ann and the new addition, Danny, and report back for active duty.

Time moved on and he was missing home and the monetary blessings he was used to receiving from his building business. I don't remember where he was, but his ship was coming near to an island. I think it was in the South Pacific. They decided to stop at this island and get off of the ship for a while. They had been instructed to stay together and not to leave the shore. There was a path leading back into the jungle, and although he had been instructed not to leave the shore, with Earl's very inquisitive mind, he just wandered down this path back into the jungle. After a little while he felt the presence of other people, and immediately he was surrounded by a group of very small native men. Of course, by now, he is remembering the words of instruction they had received before leaving the ship. "Stay on the shore. Stay together." Well, it's too late for that, he thought. I have already disobeyed those orders, so I guess I will find out what the penalty for my disobedience will be.

Suddenly, a man he assumed to be their leader stepped forward and asked him, in English, if he would like to hear them sing? He responded by saying, "I would love to hear you sing!" They began to sing a song entitled "Jesus Never Fails." It goes like this: "Jesus never fails, Jesus never fails, heaven and earth may pass away, but Jesus never fails." [10]

You talk about God showing up in your time of need or discouragement. Earl had disobeyed orders and gotten himself in a jam, but God was still looking out for him and protecting him from possible harm. The leader of this group of small men then told him that there had been a missionary who was a white man that had lived in their village and taught them about Jesus and also had taught them the song they had sung for him.

I'm not recommending that we disobey orders, but I am saying that God knows the intents of our hearts and He is available when needed. The Scripture says: For it is God which worketh in you both to will and to do of his good pleasure" (Philippians 2:13). God really has good things planned for us. He is not planning anything to hurt us but to bring us all to the point of salvation. "For the Son of man is come to seek and to save that which was lost" (Luke 19:10).

Faith and Miracles

In order for something in my life to be out of control with God, I have to make it out of control. Let me explain. To see miracles there will need to be an element of faith. If you want to have God do a miracle in your life, you need to believe He is able to perform the miracle you need done. For God to take control of your situation, you will need to let go of the controls. You also need to speak faith and never let negative words come out of your mouth.

Your faith will be tried. If you talk faith, you need to live faith. You may say you have faith that God will heal someone else, but you don't have faith for self. Faith comes when we have a relationship with God. If you want to increase your faith, start working on a greater relationship with God.

Faith comes through relationship. Relationship gives boldness to come into God's presence. Relationship opens the door for your audience with the King. Do you really believe God can do anything? Do you really believe He will do it for you?

Your faith will be tried along the way. "That the trial of your faith, being much more precious than gold that perisheth, though it be tried with fire, might be found unto praise and honor and glory at the appearing of Jesus Christ" (I Peter 1:7).

Is my faith constant, or is it sporadic? Is my faith consistent, or does it falter at every little obstacle. Is my faith strong, or is it easily discouraged? Does my faith stay focused on God, or does every little (or big) change cause my faith to hit bottom? Is my faith high and soaring one minute and the next minute it is in the proverbial tank? The New Testament writer, James, offers us direction regarding consistent faith:

> My brethren, count it all joy when ye fall into divers (of various sorts) temptations. Knowing this, that the trying of your faith worketh patience. But let patience have her perfect work, that ye may be perfect and entire, wanting nothing. If any of you lack wisdom, let him ask of God, that giveth to all men liberally, and upbraideth (of undeserved reproach) not; and it shall be given him. But let him ask in faith, nothing wavering. For he that wavereth is like a wave of the sea driven with the wind and tossed. For let not that man think that he shall receive anything of the Lord. A double minded man is unstable in all his ways.
>
> James 1: 2-8

I have mentioned previously that as you are trying your best to live a life of faith, that it is imperative that you speak positive words. Guard your words.

There have been times that I would start to say something negative, and immediately, before it escaped out of my mouth, it was like the Lord checked my spirit, and I said nothing. I am feeling very inspired here to admonish you to watch your words. Words of the person that has faith are positive words of encouragement.

How can you keep your faith in God steady? The way to keep your words positive is to stay in the Word of God and maintain a daily life of prayer. The enemy of your soul will do everything in his power to keep you from your daily time with God, and he (the devil) will continually want you to speak negative words. It will be shocking to see what these two things will do to improve your faith: prayer and Bible reading.

It will also improve your self-image when you are doing what you know is the right thing. When you bypass or just delay and put off your prayer time, you are automatically under conviction because you know that what you are doing is not what you are supposed to be doing. And to speak negatively about someone else or about things you are dealing with in your own life will automatically bring condemnation to your spirit.

An example of speaking negative would be like saying I know the Lord can do anything, but I'm not sure He will do what I need. I know He healed sister so and so, but she probably lives closer to God than I do.

I remember a time some years ago when our first granddaughter was born with a disease called non-immune fetal hydrops (more about Rachel in another chapter). Her condition was extremely serious, and she was in Riley Children's Hospital for ten weeks.

We watched as her condition deteriorated to the place that the doctors gave her no hope. It was in that setting that my wife said to me one evening, "If I thought Rachel was going to make it, I would go to the dress shop in Nashville that sells fancy little dresses and buy her one of those dresses." I said to her, "Go buy the dress." She bought the dress. A few days later Rachel pulled out the ventilator tube, and after a few more days she was wearing that dress. That was thirty six years ago. Jesus Christ the same yesterday, today and forever. Sometimes it looks like the answer is not going to come, but rest assured, if it is the will of God, it shall happen.

The Lord is my light and my salvation; whom shall I fear? The Lord is the strength of my life; of whom shall I be afraid? When the wicked, even mine enemies and my foes, came upon me to eat my flesh, they stumbled and fell. Though an host should encamp against me, my heart shall not fear; though war should rise against me, in this will I be confident. One thing have I desired of the Lord, and that will I seek after; that I may dwell in the house of the Lord all the days of my life, to behold the beauty of the Lord, and to enquire in his temple. For in the time of trouble he shall hide me in his pavilion ; in the secret of his tabernacle shall he hide me; he shall set me up upon upon a rock. And now shall my head be lifted up above mine enemies round about me: therefore will I offer in his tabernacle sacrifices of joy; yea will I sing, yea, I will sing praises unto the Lord. Hear O Lord, when I cry with my voice; have mercy also upon me, and answer me. When thou saidest, seek ye my face; my heart said unto thee, Thy face, Lord, will I seek. Hide not thy face far from me; put not thy servant away in anger: thou hast been my help; leave me not, neither forsake me, O God of my salvation. When my father and my mother forsake me, then the Lord will take me up. Teach me thy way, O Lord, and lead me in a plain path, because of mine enemies. Deliver me not unto the will of mine enemies: for false witnesses are risen up against me, and such as breatheOut cruelty. I had fainted, unless I had believed to see the goodness of the Lord in the land of the living. (Here is where faith kicks in: author's comment) Wait on the Lord: be of good courage, and he shall strengthen thine heart: wait, I say, on the Lord.

Psalms 27: 1-14

I don't think we will ever find ourselves in the dire circumstance that David found himself in the above Scriptures. His enemies sought constantly to find him so they could kill him. They would come near where he was hidden but couldn't find him. Although our situations may not be in the same category as David's, any problem we may have could be classified as very serious to us, and as the song says, "If it matters to you, it matters to the Master."[11]

In the midst of all his problems, David desires to dwell in the house of the Lord. Why does he want to dwell in the house of the Lord? He wants to see the beauty of the Lord and to be able to inquire of the Lord. He wanted to be able to ask the Lord questions. He knows also that the Lord will shelter him in his pavilion (safe place) and he would be sheltered and established soundly, where he would be able to sing praises unto the Lord. He also knows that when he cries and seeks God's face, that God will not hide his face but will be available to hear and answer his cry. Neither will the Lord forsake him. He wants the Lord to teach him and lead him in a plain (level, upright) path away from his enemies.

He prays that the Lord will not turn him over to his enemies, when false witnesses come against him, breathing out lies and cruel things. He finishes this Psalm by saying, "… wait and hope for and expect the Lord; be brave and of good courage and let your heart be stout and enduring." Yes, wait for, and hope for, and expect the Lord.

I realize there are many Scriptures concerning the subject of faith.

I also realize how difficult it is to stay faith focused. The enemy of our soul works overtime trying to keep us in the valley of doubt. As I am sitting here typing my thoughts today, I can only imagine what could happen if we could only keep our faith focused for a while.

Rachel (As told by her mother, Chris Hunter)

> I was young and pregnant with my first child. I had no experiences with difficult pregnancies or, quite honestly, the medical world at all. I grew up in a large family, but thankfully we did not have much experience with health problems, doctors, or hospitals.
>
> At about thirty-four weeks into my pregnancy I went to my obstetrician for a regularly scheduled appointment, and the doctor felt a need to do an ultrasound (this was before they did ultrasounds on every baby, but only if it was medically indicated). I was taken into another room, and I remember the nurse conducting the ultrasound, and she was very somber. She called the doctor in, and they had a whispered conversation in the corner away from the exam table I was lying on. The doctor let me know that "things did not look quite normal," and he was also concerned that my blood pressure was slightly elevated, and I was retaining a lot of fluid. I was sent home to take it easy.
>
> Several days later I was not feeling well and thought I may be having some contractions, so I called the doctor's office, and he instructed me to go to the hospital so I could be checked out. I was admitted to the hospital. Several days into my hospitalization

Finding God: My Journey Through Pancreatic Cancer

I told the nurse that I was a bit uncomfortable with back pain, so they put a monitor on to make sure I "wasn't in labor," and I was. Everything happened quickly at that point: no time for an epidural or much of any preparation, and a little baby girl was born. She came so quickly that her clavicle was broken on the way out! We named her Rachel Elena.

That sounds like a happy ending to a difficult pregnancy. However, the obstetrician knew much more than he had told me and had a transport team from Riley Children's Hospital in Indianapolis on site at the hospital in Columbus, Indiana, and they began working on my little baby girl immediately. She was not breathing and had other complications that were not diagnosed yet. They stabilized her and took her right away to downtown Indianapolis to a Neonatal Intensive Care Unit (NICU) while I remained for several days at the hospital about an hour away to be monitored and get my health stabilized. This was very difficult for a new mother and in 1984 there were no cell phones and no capability of doing a Face Time or Zoom call.

When I was released I went immediately to the hospital to see little Rachel and was shocked to see her with tubes everywhere. She was completely dependent on a ventilator to breathe, had an umbilical central line, IV, and EKG and 02 saturation monitors. Patches of her hair had been shaved to find a good vein for IVs, and it was a sight to behold for a very sheltered young lady!

She had a whole plethora of diagnoses, but her

primary diagnosis was non-immune fetal hydrops. Of course, we had never heard of this condition, and we could not "google" it back in 1984 or ask Siri, so we asked questions and tried to absorb everything we were being told by doctors and nurses, and us without any medical knowledge or education. However, to help you understand how serious this condition is, I decided to google it as I was writing this chapter and wanted to share some information I found to confirm the severity of this condition. Fetal hydrops, or hydrops fetalis, is a serious condition in which fluid builds up in two or more areas of the baby's body causing severe swelling. The condition can be fatal.[12]

The fluid may accumulate:
1. in the abdominal cavity (ascites)
2. around the lungs (pleural effusion)
3. around the heart (pericardial effusion)
4. in the skin or scalp (edema)

Another website states: "Hydrops fetalis often results in death of the infant shortly before or after delivery. The risk is highest for babies who are born very early or who are ill at birth."[13]

Rachel stayed in the NICU for 10 weeks. I could go into all of the details of everything that occurred and challenges faced but have decided to summarize the most significant and/or life threatening conditions that were likely caused by the overarching diagnosis of hydrops, although it could be argued that the multiple birth defects may have caused the hydrops.

- Malrotation of the bowel (intestinal malrotation): Rachel's intestines were

twisted causing blockage. She had surgery at about 7 weeks to correct this.
- Hypertension
- Ptosis (droopy eyelids): Rachel had surgery just before turning 5 years old to correct this.
- Tracheomalacia: This condition causes the airway to collapse while breathing, thus the reason Rachel was on a ventilator for almost 10 weeks (more about this later).

I made the hour drive to be at Rachel's bedside in the busy NICU every day except one during her 10 week hospitalization. There were high days where she was making progress, and there were low days with setbacks and lack of progress. My mother, husband, and I spent about 20 straight hours there one day when we arrived early in the morning for Rachel's surgery to correct her bowel malrotation, and it was delayed multiple times, the surgery took longer than expected, and we left the hospital around 2:00 a.m. in the morning exhausted and hungry but thankful for a successful surgery. We knew now that Rachel would be able to be given nutrition through her digestive system instead of through her veins but were still concerned that she was not able to breathe on her own without the assistance of the ventilator. All the while I sat in the nursery for hours on end and watched the nurses as they cared for all the tiny and very sick babies, and I began to become very interested in learning more about health care.

At about 9 weeks it was decided that, since they

could not get Rachel to breathe on her own due to the tracheomalacia, it would be best to do a tracheostomy and insert a tube into the trachea to keep the airway open. They were hopeful that, since she was now eating after the bowel surgery and not requiring much oxygen through the ventilator, they would be able to send her home with the tracheostomy tube that we would be taught to take care of. Of course this was not the most optimal outcome we were wanting but to be able to take Rachel home and not make the drive to Indianapolis every day did sound like a better situation. I do need to say that from Rachel's birth there was a group of people, including family and friends, that were praying across the country for her healing. My parents were praying and believing and had even demonstrated acts of faith such as buying a special dress for her first church service. My father (author of this book) told my mother to go buy the dress because Rachel was going to live. My mother was crocheting a beautiful white dedication gown hopeful that Rachel would soon wear it. Of course there were naysayers as well that would say that she would not live, but we continued to believe and put our faith in whatever the outcome was to be in God's hands.

The day arrived that Rachel was to have the tracheostomy. We were praying for the best outcome, knowing the risks, and knowing that she may have the tube in her trachea for life, years, or, the best case scenario for a brief time. We thought "maybe this is the answer to our prayers." We arrived at the hospital on the day of surgery, this time with plenty of snacks, remembering the 20-hour day a few weeks earlier, prepared to be sitting in the surgery waiting room for hours as before. When we arrived at the hospital, we had a big surprise! The nurse advised us that Rachel had decided to pull out her own ventilator tube, and they decided to see if she could breathe on her own. That had been earlier that morning, and they had not needed to put her back on the ventilator. I can't remember the exact amount of time that had passed, but it had been hours, and she was still breathing on her own, so they canceled the surgery!

I can't believe we were so surprised after all of the prayers that had gone up for little Rachel the previous 9 weeks. We thought that maybe inserting the trach and getting her home was the best that the healing was going to be. O ye of little faith! Rachel began to make great strides at that point, and within days she was transferred out of NICU, and about a day after being in a regular hospital room she was released to go home.

I'd love to say that all was perfect, that Rachel only had to go to the doctor for "well-child" visits, had no residual effects, and her life has been a bed of roses. This is not the case. Just as fighting for her life from the beginning and overcoming life-threatening challenges, she has persevered through life. She is a fighter and never quits trying. Things have not been easy. Her father has not been in her life since she was two years old, but God gave her a new daddy around her fifth birthday. It may have taken a little more effort to get through school and life, but she got her driver's license, graduated from high school, then got her Certified Nursing Assistance certification, and works as a home health aide. She has one of the best work-ethics of anyone I know.

Life is not always as we plan. God sometimes allows things in our life to mold us, to make us what we ought to be, just as the old song we used to sing in church. I know, for me, going through this life situation changed who I am. Because of this situation, along with other life changing situations I experienced several years later, I became more dependent on God, more compassionate, more understanding, and I became a Registered Nurse after sitting in NICU for ten weeks observing the nurses. I began my nursing career in NICU, worked several other areas of nursing and then moved on to a corporate career that has been a blessing to me and my family. I honestly do not believe that would have ever happened if I did not have a baby in NICU for ten weeks. All things happen for a reason. Our life situations are brought into our lives to make us better, not bitter. I have many, but one of my favorite songs is "I Never Lost My Praise." One of my favorite quotes is "Life is hard, but God is good."

More About Faith

I am not trying to tell you that I am overly endowed with faith, but I have found, through the years, that when I am facing serious situations, if I can just grab hold of simple faith, God comes through just like His Word said He would. While I was in the hospital for two weeks, and I was certainly seriously ill or they wouldn't have kept me for two weeks, I found out first-hand what it meant to have a death warrant over my head, but it was like the Lord empowered me to be able to throw out my faith anchor.

Finding God: My Journey Through Pancreatic Cancer

As I said in the first chapter, I was lying there very sick. One of the doctors had just told me that it very probably was pancreatic cancer. Any doctor will tell you that the diagnosis of pancreatic cancer is the same as giving you a death warrant. As I lay there, with all of this rolling around in my head, I literally felt no fear, although I was a bundle of emotions. What can I do to make this easier for Karen? Oh God, I have a lot of loose ends that are too large for me, let alone for Karen and the kids to take care of. If I have any choice I don't want to die, but if You choose death for me, I'm ready.

This is the moment that I have spent my whole life for. If this is "that moment" I am ready, if You will just give me time to get my natural house in order. This is the moment that I have served God all these years for, and then I prayed Hezekiah's prayer, not asking for healing but for time to set my house in order. I lay back and rested, still very ill.

Somehow my prayer penetrated the hospital floors above me, through the roof of Franciscan Hospital, journeyed through the heavenly atmosphere, and stopped somewhere out there in space where it landed at the throne of God.

He, in His great mercy, heard my prayer and sent an almost immediate answer to my prayer. My favorite Scripture found in Ephesians 3:20, "Now unto him that is able to do exceeding abundantly above all that we ask or think, according to the power that worketh in us," comes to mind as I am writing this. Literally, my favorite Scripture went to work when my prayer sped faster than a rocket through the heavenlies to the throne of God.

After ascending immediately to the throne of God, He (God) sent the answer back to Franciscan Hospital within a few hours when a servant of God, Tony Oliver, had a message that was so important to deliver that he came to the hospital on a knee scooter, with a ruptured Achilles tendon. He rolled in through the doorway and immediately proclaimed, "It's not over elder, the Lord gave me the Scriptures where Hezekiah prayed, and God extended his life fifteen years. This isn't it!!!

No, I didn't just get an answer for extended time, I got an answer that said, "Your CT scan shows no sign of cancer; you are in remission." Yes, the story is a repeat of what I wrote earlier, but I just had to repeat it again to give emphasis to what God really did. Do you get it? This is how powerful our God is. This is an amazing story, even if it is mine.

I feel like telling you that this can be your story. There is nothing special about me. I am just one of the King's kids that called out to Daddy for help, and He heard my cry and came running. I am just simple enough to believe that "He is, and that He is a rewarder of them that diligently seek him" (Hebrews 11: 6).

I found out that "if it matters to me, it matters to the master."

> Seeing then that we have a great high priest, that is passed into the heavens, Jesus the son of God, let us hold fast our profession(faith in Jesus).For we have not an high priest which cannot be touched with the feeling of our infirmities; but was in all points tempted like as we are, yet without sin.
>
> Hebrews 4:14-15

I am so happy to know that Jesus has been where I am, not only having pain, but going farther and also suffering death. So just for the record, He knows where you are today, and what you are facing, but He also knows what the outcome will be. If you will yoke up with God He will help you carry your load. "Trust in the Lord with all thine heart; and lean not unto thine own understanding. In all thy ways acknowledge him, and he shall direct thy paths" (Proverbs 3: 5-6).

I have always wanted to do what the Lord would have me do and never really prayed "Thy will be done." I realize the Bible speaks about praying according to His will, but I hardly ever prayed that exact prayer. Many times we just go ahead and do what we do without His approval. It may not be sin, and there may not be anything wrong with what we are doing, but it may not be exactly what He would have us do. "And this is the confidence that we have in him, that, if we ask anything according to his will, he heareth us: And if we know that he hear us, whatsoever we ask, we know that we have the petitions that we desired of him" (I John 5: 14-15).

I now find myself praying frequently "Thy will be done." I have realized, more so recently, that if I will actually team up with God we make an awesome team as long as we work together. If we are not working together it is not His fault, it is our fault.

When we are seeking the mind of the Lord, it is also good to have someone you can bounce your thoughts and ideas off of who will help you pray about whatever you need or whatever you intend to do for the Kingdom of God. It needs to be someone that you can trust to give you sound advice.

I find that when things I do get messed up, it is usually because I have moved ahead without the Lord's direction. Then I cry out to Him, and He helps me get things back together. It's like when you give your children sound advice about things in life that you have already experienced, but they don't listen. You want to say, "I told you so," but you just quietly watch them and hurt with them as they have to learn lessons for themselves.

I remember one time we had Irvin Baxter, from End-time Ministries, preaching at our church. He made a statement, saying, "The best way to learn something is to do it yourself, right?" I said, "Amen." He then said, "No, it is better to learn it from someone who already knows it." I found out that as human beings we think our thoughts and our ideas are always the best. I will admit, after being in business for many years, there are many business decisions I made without the Lord's council. After many years of making decisions, you kind of get the idea that you have been doing this for a long time and you know how to do it because of past knowledge. What you have done in the past has worked out okay, so you just move on with what has worked in the past.

Our business was connected to the building industry. In the building business you may have some real good customers, and things are moving along very well, but in short order, things can turn around and business can die. The year 2006 was a good example of that. We had finished 2006 with a record year. At the end of that year, our largest account decided they were going to close their Indianapolis operation. In that same time period the economy crashed. We had weathered many such situations over the years, but this one was different. I was nearing the time that I wanted to retire, so I continued working by myself and teaming up with another person, working together and sharing our work until I had liquidated all of my equipment. In hindsight, if I had run all of this by the Master, He would probably have kept me from making some of the decisions I had made.

However, it was during these latter years that God allowed Karen and me not to rebound financially, but spiritually, and have the most successful experience working in His kingdom. After what we felt was a terrible thing to happen in our latter years (the loss of our financial base), God helped us, amazingly, and we were able to do the greatest work we had ever been able to do for the Lord, the establishing of the Aurora church, in the unheard of time of five and one half years.

Finding God: My Journey Through Pancreatic Cancer

Even though it was a financial strain, I can honestly say if I had a choice in the matter, and knew what the final outcome would be, I would choose the final outcome of starting one more church, knowing that it would certainly not be the choice that would feather my financial nest but that God was going to perform the many miracles along the way with the establishment of a new church. Little did I know that in about three years I was going to need some absolute health miracles, and God was going to come through in a mighty powerful way.

Another miracle happened for us a few years ago. Karen was struggling with vertigo. Her head was spinning, and it was hard to keep her balance. For three or four months she dealt with this. It seemed that nothing she did would help her. The doctor gave her medicine to try and give her some relief, and when she took the medicine, it would completely knock her out, and she couldn't stay awake, so she quit taking it.

One evening we attended a fellowship meeting at New Albany, Indiana. It was a great service, but Karen was struggling with vertigo so extremely that she really could not enjoy the service, neither was she able to stand up without the reeling sensation. Pastor Mahurin spoke about having situations in your life that are very disturbing and there was nothing you could do to change it. The title of his message was "FED UP!"

I believe that many times these things we suffer are brought on us by the enemy of our soul. He will do anything in his power to disrupt our lives or hinder our spiritual progress. We felt like that was what was going on with Karen's situation with vertigo.

As the sermon came to a conclusion, there was an invitation given to those who were dealing with issues that were too big for them to handle, to come forward for prayer. She said she was fed up having to deal with vertigo. She stepped out into the aisle and headed toward the front. The ministry laid hands on her, as is mentioned in Mark 16:18, and immediately she was healed of vertigo.

The Bible says "… ye have not, because ye ask not" (James 4:2). Thank God we have the promise that the Lord hears when we call, and He has all power and is still able to heal. When you begin to open your heart to God and petition Him for your needs, you must have faith to believe that what He said in His Word is true, and He will do what He said He would do.

We should also have a spirit of expectancy and really believe He is going to do the thing you are praying for. If you cannot believe it is going to happen, you are just wasting your breath and energy, but if you can believe and not doubt, He will do what His Word said He would do.

My explanation of faith is: Faith is to be able to see with the eye of your mind and the Spirit of God the things that you cannot see with your natural (carnal) eye. You may not have any idea how God is going to work out your situation. To the natural eye there is no way to see it come to pass, but in your spirit you just know that it will happen.

When you are living with faith and trust in God, doubt does not just go away and hide. Doubt is always lurking around the corner, especially if you are dreaming about doing something for God. Satan is in every way opposed to anything about God. He hates God with an extreme hatred. He also hates every person who tries to do the work of the Lord. There is no hate like his hate toward people whose faith is in the Lord. Also comparative to that hatred is when you make up your mind that you are going to serve God with all of your heart. He will do everything in his power to mess you up. He will mess up anything you try to do. That is the reason you need to stay close to the Lord. I didn't say try to stay close to the Lord, I said stay close to the Lord.

When you make a commitment to live for the Lord or to do a work for the Lord, you need to understand that you just started a battle. You started a war! The good thing is if you stay up close to the Lord, the devil can't stop a "God thing." I have found through the years that as long as you are doing God's work, God's way, you are going to have opposition, but if you stay faithful to God, the enemy is helpless to stop you. He may slow you down, but he absolutely cannot stop you.

When you are filled with the Holy Spirit you have power to stand against all of the fiery darts that satan hurls in your direction.

> Finally, my brethren, be strong in the Lord, and in the power of his might. Put on the whole armor of God, that ye may be able to stand against the wiles (tricks and strategies) of the devil. For we wrestle not against flesh and blood, but against principalities, against powers, against the rulers of the darkness of this world, against spiritual wickedness in high places. Wherefore take unto you the whole armor of God, that ye may be able to withstand in the evil day, and having done all, to stand (hold your ground). Stand therefore, having your loins girt about with truth, and having on the breastplate of righteousness; And your feet shod with the preparation of the gospel of peace; Above all, taking the shield of faith, wherewith ye shall be able to quench all the fiery darts of the wicked. And take the helmet of salvation, and the sword of the Spirit, which is the word of God: Praying always with all prayer and supplication in the Spirit, and watching thereunto with all perseverance

and supplication for all saints.

Ephesians 6: 10-18

In Paul's day there was demonic activity, but I believe that in these last days we are literally wrestling against the demons of hell that have been unleashed against the servants of the most high God. That is why we must access our Spiritual weapons. We are living in days where we must be clothed with the Spirit. We are only victorious as long as we are clothed with the Spirit.

Our battles are won in the Spirit, and we must have faith that God will work with us. So you prayed and your prayer was not answered. Pray again. Don't give up. Stay the course. There is never a victory without a battle. Just keep fighting the good fight of faith.

The Faith of Noah

There are many instances in the Old Testament which are excellent examples of faith at work. In Hebrews 11 we find mention of many Old Testament stories about people who had great faith. "By faith Noah, being warned of God of things not seen as yet, moved with fear, prepared an ark to the saving of his house; by the which he condemned the world, and became heir of the righteousness which is by faith" (Hebrews 11: 7).

In Genesis 2 God created Adam and Eve and told them to be fruitful and multiply. By the time you get to Genesis 6, man had already become so wicked that God is ready to destroy his creation.

> And God saw that the wickedness of man was great in the earth, and that every imagination of the thoughts of his heart was only evil continually. And it repented the Lord that he had made man on the earth, and it grieved him at his heart. And the Lord said, I

> will destroy man whom I have created from the face
> of the earth; both man, and beast, and the creeping
> thing, and the fowls of the air; for it repenteth me that
> I have made them.
>
> Genesis 6:5

The Lord's creation, man, had made Him so angry because of his (man's) wickedness that He was going to destroy His whole creation, not only man, but all living things. That is some pretty strong anger to destroy all of His breathing creation. Does this sound anything like the day we are living in? It sounds to me like, if God looks at this world today the same as He did in Noah's day, He is probably planning our demise.

But in the midst of all the wickedness going on, God noticed that there was one man who didn't deserve to die, and that was a man named Noah. "But Noah found grace in the eyes of the Lord" (Genesis 6:8). If we could draw a parallel here, we can believe that the planned destruction of our world will also contain a clause to exempt the church of the mighty God from destruction. We have been saved and kept by God's grace and are looking for the catching away of the church. What a glorious day that will be when we are caught up to meet Him in the air.

> And God looked upon the earth, and behold, it was
> corrupt; for all flesh had corrupted his way upon the
> earth. And God said unto Noah, The end of all flesh is
> come before me; for the earth is filled with violence
> through them; and; behold, I will destroy them with
> the earth. Make thee an ark of gopher wood; rooms
> shalt thou make in the ark, and shalt pitch it within
> and without with pitch.
>
> Genesis 6: 12-14

Noah was given all the dimensions of the ark. It was to be somewhere around 450 feet long, 75 feet wide, and 45 feet high. It will have one window in the top and one door in the side. It shall be three stories high. You will bring your sons, your wife, and your sons wives with you into the ark. You will also bring two of every sort of living thing on the earth and they shall be male and female. Of fowls and birds according to their kinds, of beasts according to their kinds, of every creeping thing of the ground according to its kind—two of every sort shall come in with you that they may be kept alive. You also need to bring with you every sort of food that is eaten and gather it up and store it and it shall be food for you and for them, and Noah did according to all that God commanded him to do, he did.

I think we need to stop here and try to analyze all of the instructions God gave Noah.

First, the overwhelming job of building the ark: He had to find all of the right trees to use in the construction process. It's one thing to hear God say build this monstrous thing, but when it actually comes down to the process of building it, you are looking at a real large process. The trees had to be found, then cut down. There was no such thing as a gasoline chain saw. They probably cut the trees with some kind of hand operated cross-cut saw. To begin with, there was no gasoline, let alone the engineering ability to make a chain saw. It would be a mighty large assignment to have in the day we are living, much less back in Bible days.

After the trees were found and cut down, they had to be transported to the job site. They most likely were transported by horses or oxen. There were no trucks or tractors to move these mighty logs: simply man-power and animal-power.

Next came the project of cutting the wood to be a dimensional lumber to make the boat out of. Scaffold had to be built, nails had to be forged, possibly hammers made. It was probably only Noah and his sons who did all of the work.

The pitch had to be prepared and, probably, troweled on the thousands of square feet of surface, and you think you have been given a hard assignment of winning the lost. Floors and stalls had to be constructed inside, along with chambers built to house the occupants. When you add it all up, you will find that it was an overwhelming task to be accomplished for the salvation of eight souls.

> Which sometimes were disobedient, when once the long suffering of God waited in the days of Noah, while the ark was a preparing, wherein few, that is, eight souls were saved by water. The like figure whereunto even baptism doth also now save us (not the putting away of the filth of the flesh, but the answer of a good conscience toward God,) by the resurrection of Jesus Christ.
>
> I Peter 3: 20

Just consider all of the effort Noah put into the saving of eight souls. And there are times that we consider it a difficult task to invite someone to church, let alone teach them a Bible study. I wonder how it will feel to stand beside Noah at judgment day? We have no idea of the cost that sometimes goes into the salvation of one soul.

Besides the job of actually building the ark, there had to be the intimidation and making fun factor. "What are you doing Noah?" "I am building an ark." "What is an ark?" "An ark is a big building that will float." "Why do you want something that will float, Noah? There is no water around to float it, besides, if there was water, how would you get that thing to the water?" "The reason I want something that will float is because God told me to build it because it is going to rain." "Really Noah, who is God? God didn't talk to you, now did he Noah? What is rain?" "Rain is water coming down from the sky." "Really, I've never seen that."

Then those Noah tried to explain the process to would tell their friends to go talk to Noah. I think this "God thing has really messed his mind up. He actually thinks that water will come down from the sky, even enough rain to float that big old thing he is building there in his yard. Do you think there is such a thing as rain? If there is, do you think there would ever be enough to float that big thing?"

> These are the generations of the heavens and of the earth when they were created, in the day that the Lord God made the earth and the heavens, And every plant of the field before it was in the earth, and every herb of the field before it grew : for the Lord God had not caused it to rain upon the earth, and there was not a man to till the ground. But there went up a mist from the earth, and watered the whole face of the ground.
>
> Genesis 2: 4-6

From a natural view point this story sounds too hard to believe, but I can just hear Noah. He believed the Word of the Lord, and just kept preaching to those around him. What do you think he was preaching? Of course, he was preaching that in order to be saved from the coming judgment you would need to be on this boat before the rain came. "For if God spared not the angels that sinned, but cast them down to hell, and delivered them into chains of darkness, to be reserved unto judgment; And spared not the old world, but saved Noah, the eighth person, a preacher ,of righteousness, bringing in the flood upon the world of the ungodly" (II Peter 2:4).

According to I Peter 3:20, only eight souls were saved in Noah's ark. What were the world conditions in Noah's days? As was previously written in Genesis 6:5, the reason the Lord destroyed the world was because of wickedness: "... every imagination of the thoughts of their heart was only evil continually." The Bible also teaches that there will be the same type of judgment in the last days. Only in the last days there will not be rain of water, but as in the days of Lot it rained fire and brimstone.

> And as it was in the days of Noe (Noah), so so shall it be also in the days of the Son of Man (Jesus Christ). They did eat, they drank, they married wives, they were given in marriage, until the day that Noe entered into the ark, and the flood came, and destroyed them all. Likewise also as it was in the days of Lot; they did eat, they drank, they bought, they sold, they planted, they builded; But the same day that Lot went out of Sodom it rained fire and brimstone from heaven, and destroyed them all. Even thus shall it be in the day when the Son of man is revealed.
>
> Luke 17:26-30

Yes, it takes a measure of faith to believe that these things will happen; however, if you have a Bible, and you believe the Bible and study your Bible, you will find that this will be reality. Biblically, before the end of the world, if you are looking for a sign of the coming of the Lord, just look around you at the conditions in the world today. Jesus Christ will appear to take His church out of this world.

You hear it said many times at funerals that the person in the casket is in a better place. This is a common thought that in the end, everyone goes to heaven. I have heard this said about people who lived their whole life committing the works of the flesh according to Galatians 5:19–21.

I was asked to go with a gentleman to visit and pray for his father who was lying in bed dying. After we prayed and left his house, the man who invited me to go with him began to talk about his father. He said that he was so sad because his father had once been a very powerful preacher but had allowed himself to fall back into the things of the world.

The gentleman did pass away shortly thereafter, and I went to his funeral. At the funeral the man who a couple days before had talked about how his father had turned away from God and fallen back into the world was now telling the people what a wonderful man his father was and he was now in a better place. I can only say that I was very confused and asked myself if the man in the casket was the same man he was talking about a few days before? It is not my intention to judge the dead, but I would think that if that man had somehow come to a place of repentance, that it would have been mentioned about how, after so many years away from God, what a glorious thing it had been when he repented and made things right.

There is nowhere in the Bible that would even hint that everybody goes to heaven. I would never want to imply at a funeral that the person in the casket had gone to heaven, or a better place, unless he had a lifestyle that resembled a life lived for Christ.

The truth is that we really don't know exactly what happens immediately after death, and I don't intend to get into any big discussion about what happens. You will need to study and find your own interpretation about what happens after death. Do we who are saved go immediately to heaven? If so, I have some other questions about the catching away of the church. The Bible reads as follows:

> But I would not have you to be ignorant, brethren, concerning them which are asleep, that ye sorrow not, even as others which have no hope. For if we believe that Jesus died and rose again, even so them

also which sleep in Jesus will God bring with him. For this we say unto you by the word of the Lord, that we which are alive and remain unto the coming of the Lord shall not prevent them which are asleep. For the Lord himself shall descend from heaven with a shout, with the voice of the archangel, and with the trump of God: and the dead in Christ shall rise first: Then we which are alive and remain shall be caught up together with them in the clouds, to meet the Lord in the air: and so shall we ever be with the Lord. Wherefore comfort one another with these words.

I Thessalonians 4: 13-18

I'm sure that there are many differing opinions concerning what happens after death. There are some things mentioned in the Bible that do not have complete and clear instructions. Another one of these concerns is the time of the catching away of the bride of Christ. Is the church caught up before the tribulation period, at the middle of the tribulation, or at the end of the tribulation. I know what I believe but have refused through the years to teach what I believe as absolute because I do not find an absolute answer to what I believe or the other ideas concerning the other beliefs.

I have heard many others through the years that adamantly declare that their position about this subject is the right position. I have great respect for each one's viewpoint. I taught the different ideas about the coming of the Lord, but then I said there are some who preach pre-trib, some who preach mid-trib, and some who preach post-trib. My position is that I believe in pan-trib.

The main thing is to live your life so that you are ready to go no matter when it happens. So if you have lived your life prepared to be caught up to be with Christ, my position is that if you are living a Christ centered, holy life, everything will pan out okay.

The story is told about a gentleman that lived a very vile and evil life, and he was well known because of his lifestyle. When he died, this man's brother told the preacher he would give him a large sum of money if he would say one good thing about his brother. He said you can say anything you want to say, about how bad he was, that he was an adulterer, that he stole, but no matter how many bad things you say, in order to get the large sum of money, you have to say at least one good thing.

The day of the funeral arrived, and it was time for the preacher to give his final words. He stood up and walked to the pulpit and began to tell all of the terrible things this man had done. He is evil. He is an adulterer. He took advantage of everyone he dealt with, and there was nothing that was too awful for him to do. Looking at all of these terrible things he has done, I do need to say at least one nice thing about him. His brother is here, and compared to his brother, this man was an angel.

Still Searching

I believe that inside every human being there is an innate desire from the age of accountability that is searching for something much larger than self. There is a constant desire for something that so far has not been found. Many times the answer is right before our eyes, but because of its simplicity, we will not accept the answer because it is too simple.

By the time you have reached this part of the book, it is my sincere hope that I have said something that would help you find what you are searching for. The truth is that we are the ones that make it so hard to find God.

It is possible to have an honest and sincere heart and still be searching for God. You may have a real relationship with the Lord and still be searching for something much deeper spiritually. If that is where you are now and it seems that you are not able to go forward any farther spiritually, let's stop and take inventory of your life. I am going to ask you some questions that are pretty straight forward and are hard to admit, but if there is something clogging your spiritual conduit, you will need to get it cleaned out.

1. Are you living a life that you know is pleasing to the Lord, or are you hiding behind some doctrine which you think gives you a license to sin and still be saved?
2. Are you doing all that you know to do that is good and biblical? "Therefore to him that knoweth to do good, and doeth it not, to him it is sin" (James 4:17).
3. When was the last time you felt like God gave you spiritual direction? Was he trying to get you to make some changes in your lifestyle?
4. Was he directing you to Scriptures that were not in sync with your traditions?
5. Is tradition more important to you than God's Word?
6. Question 3 asks, when was the last time you felt like God gave you direction? The next question: Did you do what he directed you to do? If, in fact, you haven't followed His direction, what makes you think He is going to move you along any farther if you have not submitted to his previous direction?

Do you feel like your will is more important than God's will for your life? You may sincerely believe that you are doing the right thing, but there has been a nagging little feeling that you need to forget about your personal feelings and allow God to do what he has been trying to do in your life with no cooperation on your part.

We find a very good illustration of a person who was doing right according to all he had been taught by the religious leaders of that day. It was none other than Saul traveling the road to Damascus.

> And Saul, yet breathing out threatenings and
> slaughter against the disciples of the Lord, went
> unto the high priest, And desired of him letters to
> Damascus to the synagogues, that if he found any
> of this way, whether they were men or women, he
> might bring them bound unto Jerusalem. And as he
> journeyed, he came near to Damascus: and suddenly
> there shined round about him a light from heaven:
> And he fell to the earth, and heard a voice saying to
> him, Saul, Saul, why persecutest thou me? And he
> said, who art thou, Lord? And the Lord said, I am
> Jesus whom thou persecuetest: it is hard for thee to
> kick against the pricks.
>
> Acts 9: 1-5

What the Lord was talking about was evidently something that He had been trying to get through to Saul, but Saul had been moving along at a steady pace to do what his religious leaders had wanted done. The illustration the Lord used was "… it is hard for thee to kick against the pricks" (Acts 5:5). This was an expression that came from a Greek proverb. The Jews that had been educated in the schools of Tarsus might have read them from the Greek poets. What they taught was that to resist a power altogether superior to our own is a profitless and perilous experiment. The more sharply the goad pricks, the more the ox struggled against it. An ox goad was a sharp piece of iron stuck into the end of a stick that is used to urge the ox on. Among the Hebrews these goads were made very large, and the more the ox fought against it, the harder he was prodded with the goad to move forward in the direction he was being steered to go.

Hence we find that Saul had an experience in which his conscience had probably been pricked when he watched Stephen being stoned, but he did not allow his conscience to focus on the wrong that he had done but to just forge ahead with his despicable hatred of Jesus.

> Then they cried out with a loud voice, and stopped their ears, and ran upon him with one accord, And cast him out of the city, and stoned him: and the witnesses laid down their clothes at a young man's feet, whose name was Saul. And they stoned Stephen, calling upon God, and saying, Lord Jesus, receive my spirit. And he kneeled down, and cried with a loud voice, Lord, lay not this sin to their charge. And he fell asleep.
>
> Acts 9: 1-5

I would think it would be hard to watch as a man was being stoned, and as they threw the stones the man being stoned would pray that the Lord would not charge this great sin to their account, but now it was time for Saul to face the wrong that he had been involved in and get his punishment.

> And he trembling and astonished said, Lord, what wilt thou have me to do? And the Lord said unto him, Arise, and go into the city, and it shall be told thee what thou must do. And the men which journeyed with him stood speechless, hearing a voice, but seeing no man. And Saul arose from the earth; and when his eyes were opened, he saw no man: but they led him by the hand, and brought him into Damascus. And he was three days without sight, and neither did eat nor drink. And there was a certain disciple at Damascus, named Ananias, and to him said the Lord in a vision, Ananias . And he said, behold I am here, Lord. And the Lord said unto him, arise and go into the street which is called Straight, and inquire in the house of Judas for

one called Saul, of Tarsus: for behold he prayeth, And hath seen in a vision a man named Ananias coming in, and putting his hand on him, that he might receive his sight. Then answered Ananias, Lord, I have heard by many of this man, how much evil he hath done to thy saints at Jerusalem: And here he hath authority from the chief priest to bind all that call on thy name. But the Lord said unto him, go thy way: for he is a chosen vessel unto me, to bear my name before the gentiles, and kings, and the children of Israel: For I will show him how great things he must suffer for my name's sake. And Ananias went his way, and entered into the house; and putting his hands on him said, Brother Saul, the Lord, even Jesus, that appeared unto thee in the way as thou camest, hath sent me, that thou mightest receive thy sight, and be filled with the Holy Ghost. And immediately there fell from his eyes as it had been scales: and he received sight forthwith, and arose, and was baptized. and when he had received meat, he was strengthened. Then was Saul certain days with the disciples which were at Damascus. And straightway he preached Christ in the synagogues, that he is the Son of God.

Acts 9: 6-20

I truly believe that Saul thought he was doing God a great service as he was persecuting and killing the saints of God. He was truly searching for God but was following the direction of the wrong leader. Today many people are searching for God and following leaders who are not leading them into full truth. If we believe that the New Testament church was established on the day of Pentecost in the Book of Acts, how is it that we have strayed so far from the teachings of the Book of Acts?

Finding God: My Journey Through Pancreatic Cancer

The Book of Acts church was a vibrant, exciting, and powerful church. They prayed and were in one accord, and when they prayed the place was shaken as the Holy Ghost swept into that room. I am praying that if you have not received the Holy Ghost, that the Holy Ghost will sweep into your life with great power and authority and place something within your heart that will cause a great change and lead you by the hand into your place of ministry.

Hopefully in your journey to find God, I pray that by now you have opened yourself up to allow the Holy Ghost to give you direction. Don't resist God's direction but open your heart to the leading of His Spirit. Don't force your way forward as Saul did to be able to find the God that you are searching for. It may be uncomfortable for you to change and become what God is trying to create in you, but if you are truly searching for God to open the door of your heart and life and allow Him to do whatever He is trying to do with you, just go ahead and open the door.

I believe Saul truly had a heart that wanted to please God but was so wrapped up in his tradition that he really couldn't understand what God wanted him to do. Even with a nagging conviction working inside him after watching Stephen being stoned to death, he just blundered forward doing the same things he had always done.

It is my opinion that God had been trying for a good while to get Saul's attention but for some reason or other Saul was not hearing what God was really saying to him, and he just kept bull-dogging his way along the same old path which he had been traveling. I don't believe God would use such drastic measures to change someone's course on His first attempt to reach them.

In my mind I can see God using much less drastic measures. He would probably start with a still small voice just trying to get Saul to slow down and listen. Then when Saul watched as Stephen was stoned, his conscience was being pricked about the injustice of a man being killed just because of his personal convictions about salvation.

I somehow believe that when watching a man die didn't make Saul pay attention and listen, then there began to be warning signs and sounds trying to get his attention. Next there would be red lights and alarms going off in his spirit, but that never so much as slowed him down in his persecution of the church. Jesus evidently saw Saul's potential and never stopped trying to get him to change his ways.

Saul was so blinded by tradition and hatred that he wasn't able to recognize what God was really trying to do with him, so in order to get his eyes opened, God had to first make him blind. In Saul's blindness, Jesus said, I have tried to do this a better way, but your stubbornness has forced me to use the last resort. It was through his blindness that his eyes were opened, and he found the light of the truth in Jesus Christ. If you are struggling and uncomfortable with whatever God is trying to do with your life, just relax for a while, find a place where you can get alone with God, and listen for the still small voice of Jesus. Believe me, you will know when He speaks.
I will promise you that it is better to be able to hear God without Him having to use drastic measures to get your attention. According to I Samuel 15:22, "to obey is better than sacrifice."

Open the Gate

There is a story found in Acts 12 that I find quite interesting. The Bible says that Herod stretched forth his hand to vex the church. In doing so he killed James with the sword, and because it pleased the Jews, he proceeded further to take Peter also.

And when he had apprehended him, he put him in prison and had four quaternions (four squads of four) of soldiers to guard him and intended to bring him to the people after Easter. So Peter was kept in prison; but fervent prayer was made unto God continually for him by the church. The very night before Herod was going to bring him forth, Peter was sleeping between two soldiers, fastened with two chains, and had guards who were guarding the door of the prison. Suddenly an angel of the Lord appeared and was standing beside Peter, and a light shined in the place where he was. The angel gently tapped Peter on the side and woke him up. He then told him to get up quickly. And when he did, the chains fell off of his hands.

Then the angel told him to tighten his belt and put his shoes on, which he did. Then the angel told him to put on his outer garment and follow him. And Peter went out following along after the angel, not really knowing what was going on with the angel but thought he was seeing a vision.

When they had passed the first and second guard, they came to an iron gate which led out into the city. When they approached the gate it opened up by itself like a modern gate with an automatic eye. Of course, there was no such thing as an automatic eye, but what they were seeing was a miracle in action. God knows all about your circumstances and according to Luke 1: 37, "For with God nothing shall be impossible."

When the gate opened by itself, they were out in the city. They passed one street, and the angel disappeared. Then Peter said to himself (A miraculous deliverance like that would make you talk to yourself.), "Now I know and am sure that the Lord has sent His angel and delivered me from the hand of Herod and also from the Jewish people who intended to harm me."

When Peter finally realized what was going on, after considering all that had happened, he went to the house of Mary, John Mark's mother, and found a large number of people who had gathered there praying. Peter was going to be executed the next day, and the Bible says that prayer was made without ceasing for Peter's release.

Since Peter was supposed to be put to death the next day, this large number of people were gathered together in prayer interceding for him. As the people prayed, God sent an angel to answer their prayer, and the method used was what we would call a jail break. This is a wonderful story about how God will take care of His people.

Just take a close look at these circumstances. Peter is in prison. Not only is he in prison, he has sixteen guards to keep him from escaping. He is secured by two chains and the sixteen soldiers, plus the keepers of the prison doors. He is sleeping between two soldiers. An angel comes in and tells Peter to rise quickly, and when he stands up, the chains fall off. Either the guards were in a very deep sleep or the chains never made a noise as they fell off. Either way is a miracle. Chains are not silent when they are moved, let alone when they are dropped. You cannot move a chain without it making a noise.

The angel speaks to Peter, telling him to put on his coat, and still the guards never heard a word. Peter still believes that he is having a dream. They went through two wards and came to an iron gate that opened automatically, and the angel and Peter walked through without any interference. The angel continues to lead him, and when they passed the first street, the angel immediately disappeared and left him.

Then reality sets in, and Peter realizes that this is not a dream or a vision but that God had, indeed, sent an angel to deliver him from the hand of Herod and from all that the Jewish people had planned to do to him. When he became aware of what had happened and understood all of the elements of his case, he went to the house of Mary, the mother of John Mark, where there was a large number of people that had gathered together to pray for him. As he was knocking at the gate, a young lady named Rhoda came to the gate. She recognized Peter's voice, and in her excitement, she failed to open the gate but ran in and told those praying that Peter was at the gate. They told her that she was crazy, but she insisted that it was true, Peter really was at the gate. They were saying that can't be Peter. He is in prison. That has to be his angel. I think it is ironic that they had a large group of people assembled together praying for Peter's release from prison, and now he is standing at the gate trying to get inside, but they can't believe he is actually there. They are telling Rhoda that Peter can't be at the gate because he is in prison. That has to be his angel at the door.

But Peter is still at the gate knocking and trying to get someone to open the gate and let him in. While all of this was going on inside, Peter continued to knock, and when they opened the gate and saw him, they were amazed. But Peter beckoned unto them with his hand to be quiet, and he told them the story about how the Lord had brought him out of the prison.

We may look at this story and laugh about all of these things that were going on. We say, "If I had been there I would have immediately opened the door and allowed Peter to come inside. I would never have allowed him to stand outside and knock. After all, you know, that was the reason we were there praying. We were praying for his release from prison."

Many times God is trying to guide or direct us, to help us, or give us spiritual guidance. We pray for God to help and direct us, but when He gives direction, we refuse to open the gate of our mind to be able to comprehend and follow His direction. Many times the reason we don't open the gate is because the answer He gives is not the answer we wanted to hear. If we are spiritually minded, we will accept God's guidance, but if we are locked up in tradition, we don't want to hear something that we do not believe or have been taught differently. After all, the Bible tells us that there are false teachers.

Meanwhile, the Lord stands at the gate of our heart and, like Peter, He continues to knock. We hear the knock at our spiritual door, but because we do not agree with the direction we are getting, we allow God to stand outside and knock. How long does He have to knock before we acknowledge that He is there?

I wonder how we will feel when we stand before the Lord and He questions us about why we did not open our heart's door and allow Him to answer the prayer for direction that we had prayed for? We need to ask ourselves this question. Is what I believe biblically correct or am I so locked up by tradition that I cannot move along any farther biblically without having to break fellowship with the group that I fellowship? I can see that there are certain things in God's Word that I have not acknowledged as truth because of my tradition.

I feel so inspired by God to press a little further about the traditions of man.

Tradition:
- Tradition is the transmission of customs or beliefs from generation to generation, or the fact of being passed on in this way.
- An inherited, established, or customary pattern of thought, action, or behavior (such as a religious practice or social custom).
- A belief or story or a body of beliefs or stories relating to the past that are commonly accepted as historical though not verifiable.
- The handing down of information, beliefs, and customs by word of mouth or by example from one

generation to another without written instructions.

Tradition theologically:
- Tradition is a doctrine believed to have divine authority though not in Scriptures. "Search the scriptures; for in them ye think ye have eternal life: and they are they which testify of me" (John 5: 39).
- The Amplified Bible says it this way: "You search and investigate and pore over the Scriptures diligently, because you suppose and trust that you have eternal life through them. And these very Scriptures testify about Me!" (John 5:39).

Even though God's Word does not agree with man's word (tradition), we take man's word over God's Word. I have had people say to me, "I see what the Bible is saying, but that is not what I have been taught." We have too many examples in Scripture of people walking away from tradition for us to remain in our own.

We were having a home Bible study with a large family in the area where we had started a new church. There were four adults and one young lady in this study group. They were a delightful family to teach. We had become friends, and they would visit the church regularly. As we taught the lesson, you could see that they were receiving the Word.

When we got into the Book of Acts, they excitedly accepted the fact that the New Testament church received the Holy Ghost and spoke in another language. They could accept the fact that this was true. They also accepted the fact that according to Acts 1:12-14, the disciples and Mary the mother of Jesus were in the upper room and received the Holy Ghost.

In the next week's lesson we taught about baptism, citing the many instances where they were baptized in the name of Jesus, or in the name of the Lord Jesus Christ. As I was teaching the lesson, one of the ladies looked at the others and acknowledged that she saw the truth of baptism in Jesus Name and asked the others what they were going to do about it. They came to the conclusion that they felt as though their previous baptism was good enough. I still love these people and mourn the fact that I was not able to get them baptized in Jesus Name.

That is what tradition does for people. It is like having a vaccination. A vaccination gives the recipient just enough of a germ to keep them from getting the real thing.

In another Bible study with a minister of another church denomination, I was teaching about receiving the Holy Ghost. Of course the common thought among mainstream religion is that you receive the Holy Ghost when you accept Christ as your personal Savior. They readily see that when the Holy Ghost fell on the day of Pentecost that they all spoke with tongues; however, they have been taught that the tongues experience is not necessary for them today. As I taught about receiving the Holy Ghost, evidenced by speaking with tongues, he acknowledged that he saw that experience in the Book of Acts but said, "I could not see myself speaking with tongues." How is it that we can see Bible truths but don't believe that those same truths are necessary for us today?

It grieves my heart that there are people who hear the truth of God's Word but will not accept it because of tradition and peer pressure. This is not an assault on me but against the Savior and His Word. How great it would be if we would see His truth and would open the gate to the Word and accept it! How simple: just open the gate and allow Him entrance into our heart!

We need to invite the living God into the equation of our life. The only way forward is to have a new and biblical connection with the living Christ. We desperately need Him to lead and guide us through these last days. I can assure you that if you stand before God unprepared, you will be so sorry that you placed more value on friends and tradition than upon the Word of the Lord.

I believe we have entered the era considered to be the last days. God has been patiently trying to give us the spiritual direction that we need, and it grieves His heart that we keep our heart's door locked to anything that does not coincide with our tradition. He desires to lead and guide us into deeper and fuller truth.

We do not need new concepts of doing church. WE NEED GOD! We need an old fashioned Book of Acts Pentecostal revival!

We don't need sermonizing: we need to hear from God. We need preachers that are not afraid to preach the Word with a great big heart of love and compassion. If we truly desire to have God's direction, He is desiring to give us His help and direction if we come to the point where we are willing to pray "thy will be done." The way forward is to give Him absolute power and authority to direct our lives as He sees fit. Open the gate!

If we really want His direction, we need to repent of our stubbornness, follow His direction, and open our hearts to be able to hear what the Spirit is saying to the church. We need to cry out to God and forget all of our man-made ideas and let Him lead us by His Spirit.

God never came on the scene for the children of Israel in Egyptian bondage until they began to cry out. They were only delivered when they finally realized they were in bondage and started crying out to God. They came to a point in their lives when the persecution began that they finally realized the years they had stayed in Egypt had gone from a time of respite from the famine in their home country to a time of slavery in a far country.

According to Genesis 45:6 the Israelites were only supposed to stay in Egypt for five years, until the famine that brought them to Egypt was over, but due to all the good things they received because of Joseph, they continued living there for four hundred and thirty years.

The Bible says that now there arose up a new king over Egypt, which knew not Joseph (Exodus 1:8), and he made their lives bitter with hard labor in making brick and building cities. As their lives began to be overly controlled by the Egyptian task masters, they finally realized that they were no longer free people as they had previously been. When they finally realized that they had become servants, they began to cry out to God by reason of their bondage.

Isn't that just like people today? They go their own way and do their own thing, never thinking about what the end result will be. When it is too late, they then realize that they are in bondage and are not able to help themselves. Many die in a state of bondage because of the choices that they made when they still had control of their lives. When the children of Israel finally realized the condition they were in, they began to cry out to God for deliverance.

> And it came to pass in the process of time, that the king of Egypt died: and the children of Israel sighed by reason of the bondage, and they cried, and their cry came up unto God by reason of the bondage. And God heard their groaning, and God remembered his covenant with Abraham, with Isaac, and with Jacob. And God looked upon the children of Israel and God had respect unto them.
>
> Exodus 2: 23-25

God had deliverance prepared for them by a very unlikely source.

Finding God: My Journey Through Pancreatic Cancer

That source was a stuttering shepherd on the back side of a desert. God has our personal deliverer waiting to be dispatched when we are ready to receive Him. He has already been dispatched and is ready, but He cannot come until we call for Him. He will not come until we are ready and cry out to Him, and not before we are ready.

We need to arrive at an attitude that it's not about me, it's about inviting the Holy Ghost to do what He is wanting to do. When we make up our minds that we are ready to accept His will for our lives, He shows up.

We may be going to church, serving God to a certain extent, praying for release, praying for direction, praying for hope, praying for help, and expect God to do what we are praying about while we just continue to travel in the same direction we have been traveling. God may not want to move in the direction we are asking Him for. That's why it is necessary to submit to His will. That is like doing the same old thing that you have always done and expecting a different result. "If you always do what you've always done, you'll always get what you always got."[14]

If God is not answering, maybe YOU should do what He has been knocking on your gate to get you to do and allow Him to come in and be King of your life. The answer very well could be standing just outside your gate waiting for you to open up, and you just let Him stand outside in the cold.

I would suggest that if you are praying for God to answer a certain prayer for you, and you continue having this nudging in your spirit to go in a direction that you don't especially like, maybe it is time to open the gate and allow God to answer your prayer. Your answer is very possibly within reach: open the gate.

God had the children of Israel's answer ready and waiting when

121

they finally realized that they were in trouble. When they cried out to God, then God activated the process of deliverance. We find the process God used in Exodus 3: 1-10:

> Now Moses kept the flock of Jethro his father in-law, the priest of Midian: and he led the flock to the backside of the desert, and came to the mountain of God, even to Horeb. And the angel of the Lord appeared to him in a flame of fire out of the midst of a bush: and he looked, and, behold, the bush burned with fire, and the bush was not consumed. And Moses said, I will now turn aside, and see this great sight, why the bush is not burnt. And when the Lord saw that he turned aside to see, God called unto him out of the midst of the bush, and said, Moses, Moses. And he said, Here am I. And he said, draw not nigh hither: put off thy shoes from off thy feet, for the place whereon thou standest is holy ground. Moreover he said, I am the God of thy father, the God of Abraham, the God of Isaac, and the God of Jacob. And Moses hid his face: for he was afraid to look upon God. And the Lord said, I have surely seen the affliction of my people which are in Egypt, and have heard their cry by reason of their taskmasters; for I know their sorrows; And I am come down to deliver them out of the hand of the Egyptians, and to bring them up out of that land unto a good land and a large, unto a land flowing with milk and honey; unto the place of the Canaanites, and the Hittites, and the Amorites, and the Perizites, and the Hivites, and the Jebusites. Now therefore, behold, the cry of the children of Israel is come unto me: and I have also seen the oppression wherewith the Egyptians oppress them. Come now therefore, and I will send thee unto Pharaoh, that thou mayest bring forth my people the

Finding God: My Journey Through Pancreatic Cancer

children of Israel out of Egypt.

Exodus 3: 1-10

The deliverer that God had prepared was certainly not what would have been expected. This deliverer had a lonely job keeping the flock of his father-in-law Jethro, the priest of Midian. His job had taken him to the back side of the desert. While attending to the job of watching the sheep, an angel of the Lord appeared to him in a flame of fire out of a bush. This was not a normal situation in that although the bush was burning, it was not consumed by the fire. This piqued Moses' interest because of the mysteriousness of the bush not being consumed by the fire. I can just see Moses as he watched and when the bush should have been consumed by the flames, it was still standing there just like it had always been. I can imagine the big WOW that escaped from his lips. Evidently this was such a strange occurrence that it had Moses talking to himself, or maybe he was talking to the sheep. He said, "I will now turn aside and see this great sight, why the bush is not burned up."

Could it be that many times God would like to talk to us, but we are too busy and think we don't have time to be bothered? We have been praying about a certain situation that was going on in our life, hoping that, somehow, God will give us audience and extend His golden scepter of acceptance to us so we can come into His presence. But when God takes the time to talk to us we are too busy to stop what we are doing and enter into His presence, or maybe we are not sensitive to what God is trying to do and our window of opportunity slams closed for the time being, maybe to never open again. What would it feel like to miss our appointment with God and never have another opportunity to have an audience with God?

I can only imagine what it would have been like to miss our last opportunity to start another church. If we had not responded to the call, we would have missed out on one of the greatest experiences of our lives. Not so with Moses. His thinking was that this is such a strange occurrence that I probably should stop and take a look, and just maybe this will turn out to be interesting. Because of his interest, the Bible says he turned aside to see. We can only imagine what would have happened if he had not been interested enough to make the effort and go out of his way to check out what was going on.

By the same token, I wonder what we are missing by not finding out what God has for us. Could it be that there is a town that needs a church, as our last church in Aurora, Indiana. Someone had been praying for a church in that area. Perhaps there are people who have not had the wonderful experience of receiving the baptism of the Holy Ghost, understanding baptism in Jesus name, and who are waiting for you to hear from God. I would hate to think that there are people who could have been saved if only I had been more sensitive in finding God's will for my life. Oh, God, please don't allow me to miss an opportunity that would allow someone else to hear about your love, your compassion, your mercy, and the opportunity to be filled with the Holy Ghost.

Moses had no idea what was about to happen when he stepped aside to see what he called a great sight. Little did he expect this great sight to be a great voice that would speak to him about a great opportunity to be used by God. I might add that there is nothing in this world that compares to being used by God.

So Moses stopped everything he was doing and stepped over to check out this unusual situation that was going on, and when the Lord saw that he was interested, He spoke to him out of the bush. Not only did He speak to Moses from the bush, but He called Moses by name, which brings me to another point.

Sometimes in our humanness we think that God doesn't have any idea who we are, much less know our name. The truth is that God really does know, not only who we are, but He knows everything there is to know about us. He knows how many hairs we have on our head, He knows our address, He knows if we really love Him and have a desire to please Him or if we are on an ego trip and our life is all about self.

According to the first book that I wrote, *It's Not About Me, A Life About Him,* my prayer is that when I stand before God that He will agree with the title of my book. I have truly desired for my life to portray Jesus Christ and that I can stand in the background and simply point someone else to Him. There is a statement that I often make when I step to the pulpit: "When the lights are turned off tonight, I want to have been part of the process that God uses to help someone see God through eyes of faith." That really is my desire, that if I can help someone along the way, then my living will not be in vain.

So as Moses drew near, the Lord spoke to him out of the midst of the bush. The Lord said, "Do not come near, put your shoes off your feet because the place where you stand is holy ground."

He continued to talk out of the bush and said, "I am the God of your father, the God of Abraham, the God of Isaac, and the God of Jacob." And Moses, recognizing the voice and acknowledging the fact that he understood who this God was that was talking to him, hid his face, for he was afraid to look at God. And the Lord said, "I have surely seen the affliction of My people who are in Egypt, and have heard their cry because of their taskmasters and oppressors; for I know their sorrows and sufferings and trials."

Notice where Moses was when God appeared to him. He was on the back side of the desert. When I think about "the back side of the desert," I think of a place that is God forsaken, lonely, without much to look forward to and no hope that tomorrow is going to be much different than today, or yesterday, or last week, or last month, or even perhaps the last few years.

Maybe that is the way you feel. There isn't much going on in your life. Your life is pretty mundane, certainly nothing exciting, nothing to look forward to. God said:

1. (I have seen). God said I have surely seen the affliction of my people which are in Egypt. This Scripture lets us see that God is interested in the things that pertain to all of His people. It is not just about certain big name people but about the cares and trials of each person individually. If we can get it in our heads that he really cares about each one on a personal basis then we can come boldly to the throne of grace to find our help.

2. (I have heard). This lets us know that He is continually listening to hear what is going on in our lives. How wonderful it is to know that He is listening for our voice. He is saying give me a call. I am waiting to hear your voice.

3. (I know). If He has seen, and if He has heard, that means that He knows and is waiting for us to check in and talk with Him.

4. (I have come). Knowing all about us He then comes in answer to our call. You may feel that you do not matter to Jesus, but I assure you that you DO matter, and He is available if we come to Him on His terms.

Because of the cry of the Israelite people for God to help in their time of trouble, God called Moses to leave leading the sheep to lead the people out of bondage.

Finding God: My Journey Through Pancreatic Cancer

Because of Moses' concern about a bush that was on fire but not burned up, we find a stuttering shepherd from the back side of the desert standing before Pharaoh demanding the king to let the Israelites leave from being servants in Egypt and go into the wilderness and worship their God.

Because of their cry for help, God empowered Moses to stand before Pharaoh with his rod and perform many miracles.

In the story I have just tried to relate to you, God did, in fact, see, He did hear, He did know, and He came to help those who had cried out to Him. Because He heard and responded, we have the story of Moses, the stuttering shepherd leading the children of Israel as they walk through the Red Sea on dry ground.

When we begin to cry out to God in behalf of our circumstances, out persecutions, our hopes, our needs, or other things that may be going on in our lives, He does, indeed, hear and is concerned about everything that concerns us. As I stated in a previous chapter, if it matters to you, it matters to the master. If it matters to the master, why are we nervous or overly concerned about all of these issues of life? "Casting all your care upon him; for he careth for you" (I Peter 5: 7).

Spiritual Holding Pattern

I have tried to relate some biblical references where, because of your faith in God, you are seeing some wonderful results. I have also related some of our family's personal trials and victories, all for the purpose of building your faith high enough so that you would throw out your own faith anchor and allow yourself to believe that God really does have a plan for your life. "For I know the thoughts that I think toward you, saith the Lord, thoughts of peace, and not of evil, to give you an expected end. Then shall ye call upon me, and ye shall go and pray unto me , and I will hearken unto you. And ye shall seek me, and find me, when ye shall search for me with all your heart" (Jeremiah 29:11–13).

Following is Jeremiah 29:11 from the Amplified Bible: "For I know the thoughts and plans that I have for you, says the Lord, thoughts and plans for welfare and peace and not for evil, to give you hope in your final outcome."

God already has your future planned out. Have you received what you believed were instructions from God? Do you have any idea what He wants of you? If you have received instructions, have you acted on the instructions you have been given? If you have not done what you were instructed, what makes you think you will receive more instructions?

I have written this book in answer to someone's prayer and to verify what God has been speaking to you about, and to let you know it is time to follow His exact plan—His exact instructions. God has been speaking to you and you have been bargaining with God and then going ahead and doing things your own way. God's direction requires absolute exact obedience. God is the final authority.

You are not the finished product today. Whatever stage you are at today is the beginning of God's process to bring you to the place where He can use you. His plan for you today may seem to you like a bitter pill. For God's sake, take the pill and continue in the will of God.

When you arrive at your next stage of the will of God, He will move you to the next step. Some people never achieve their full potential because they never commit to the step they are on. (God has a plan for your life.) For God's sake, submit to the Master Planner! Some people have "a like to" but never "a want to" that is so overwhelming that it will literally propel them into God's perfect will.

Finish the spiritual grade you are in so He can promote you to the next level. Don't be like the mentally challenged child that can only go so far but is not able to move to the next level. You can do it. Submit your will and graduate to the next level. It will also have challenges that you may not like, but just meet the challenges and move on.

I hate to have to tell you this, but whatever step of the will of God you are on will also have challenges of its own. That is why it is necessary to stay as clay in the Master Potter's hands. Serving God is a never ending process of challenges.

The plan of God is a never ending process of spiritual growth:
- The plan of God takes time for growth just as it takes a child time to grow.
- It requires spiritual growth.
- It requires dedication: an everyday commitment to His plan.
- If you really want to complete God's will in your life, it will require complete submission to His will. We want the graduation certificate without having gone through elementary school.
- We want the new car but don't want to pay for it.
- Let me tell you from experience that anything worth having is going to cost you something.
- After you have committed to the first things (time, spiritual growth, submission) and graduated from the first grade, then, and only then does the process move forward.

The natural, real life, growing process takes time, and the real spiritual life also takes time, so make the best of the step you are on.

The process ladder you are on now has numerous steps. Learn the lessons of the steps you are on today. It is part of the process. God has a hard time keeping us on course long enough to graduate. If you do not stay the course, there will be no graduation ceremony.

It's time to get a CAN DO spirit and get serious with God and crucify the flesh so you can do whatever God is trying to do through you.

You have searched for God and, seemingly, have not found Him. You have searched the Scriptures and feel as though the heavens are brass. There has, in your mind, been no penetration of the heavens that has propelled you to the next level. But by the time you have read this far, it is my hope that you might have picked up a nugget that has helped you move up to the next level spiritually. I hope I have either challenged you, or if necessary aggravated you, to the place that you have started your process to move up to the next spiritual level.

After much prayer trying to find an appropriate way to bring the subject of "Finding God" to a conclusion, I feel like telling you that your life is a miracle in the making. I have told you my personal story of finding God in my time on the back side of the desert. I will also admit that even though I have been a pastor for many years that this deep valley, and the experience of finding God in a new way has moved me up to a new spiritual level. The valley was certainly worth the reward.

Maybe you still feel as though you are on the back side of the desert. Maybe you feel like you have not moved forward in your spiritual experience. Perhaps you still feel like you are in a spiritual holding pattern and have not as yet received your landing instructions, and you are about to run out of fuel as you just circle the airport waiting for your time to land. Please allow me to give some final advice. While in fervent prayer this morning, God impressed me to tell you that if you feel like you have done all that you know to do and still haven't found God, that maybe you are dealing with a spirit of unforgiveness. Is there someone in your life that has hurt you or done something hurtful to you and you have never forgiven them? I know it is very difficult to forgive someone, but the Scriptures tell us we must forgive.

I have made it a practice that if I have had any kind of an issue with someone, whether it is a disagreement or a hurtful word, the first time I see that person I do my best to make it right. Having a spirit of unforgiveness locks both you and the other person in prison. "And forgive us our debts, as we forgive our debtors ... For if ye forgive men their trespasses, your heavenly Father will also forgive you: But if ye forgive not men their trespasses, neither will you Father forgive your trespasses" (Matthew 6:12,14-15). I don't know about you, but I want to be sure that my heavenly Father will forgive me.

Kate Megase, MBACP accredited Psychotherapist, Couples Counsellor and Supervisor states:

> Unforgiveness is when you are unwilling or unable to forgive someone for hurting, betraying, breaking your trust or causing you intense emotional pain. Forgiving is highly recommended, as there are various researches that have been carried out which shows that unforgiveness causes health issues including:
> - Cancer—61% of cancer patients have forgiveness issues.
> - Suppressed anger—people who often get angry for any reason have issues associated with forgiveness.
> - Low self-esteem—lack of selflove stems from not forgiving yourself or self-acceptance.

- Bitterness increases the risk of depression.
- Constant worrying increases the risk of sleep deprivation and anxiety.
- Blood pressure problems.
- Heart disease.

When someone has hurt or disappointed you, the logical response would be to think that you are hurting them by not forgiving them and holding a grudge. The harsh truth is that you are actually causing yourself more pain by holding on to the anger, and the person that you wish not to forgive has the subconscious power to control you. However, you can get disconnected from the power of control when you forgive.

How to Learn to Forgive

Decide

When you feel like you have been hurt intensely by someone close to you, it's very hard to even begin to consider forgiving them, as you want them to feel the pain. However, the first step is to release the emotional pain by making a conscious decision to forgive and let go. This process may take time, due to different emotions that you have to process.

Letting go of the baggage

True forgiveness is when you forgive and forget. However, we are imperfect human beings and although we may forgive, we may not always forget, as there may be incidents where we are triggered or reminded of past events. Even if it is a struggle to forget, it is very important to forgive by letting go of the emotional pain that has been caused.

Finding God: My Journey Through Pancreatic Cancer

Take responsibility for the part that you played

You can never control anyone: the only person that you can control is yourself. Taking responsibility for how you allowed someone to hurt you enables you to set boundaries so you don't put yourself in the same situation again.

Forgive yourself

It's easier to forgive others when you learn to forgive yourself. No one can truly hurt you deeply unless you allow them. Sometimes it is easier to blame others for causing you pain. However, the depth of the pain depends on the boundaries that you set within your relationships. Forgive yourself for allowing others to treat you with disrespect or emotional pain.

Awareness

Be aware of the negative emotions that you feel toward the other person, including: anger, bitterness, hurt, hatred, and jealously. Awareness will help you to acknowledge the need to forgive. Holding on to the negative emotions is highly toxic and not good for your health.

Acceptance

You don't need to make excuses for the person that hurt you. Even if you don't want them back in your life, it's essential to accept how you feel and the fact that you can't change the past.

Learn from experience

Sometimes we have to go through negative and painful experiences to learn some life lessons, which helps to develop ourselves. In every negative experience, it's very important to ask yourself, what lessons have you learned? This will enable you to avoid repeating the same thing over and over again. If you keep doing the same thing and don't learn from the painful experiences, then you will experience the same thing (pain) in your life. Life is like a classroom, and people are teachers, and they come into our lives to teach certain things about ourselves. So take the time to learn the lessons regardless of how painful it may be.

Talk about it

When you are ready to forgive, make arrangements to contact the person that has hurt you and express yourself. Talking things over helps you to let go.

Closure

If you have decided that you no longer want to have the person that has hurt you back in your life, then that is fine. You can write a letter to that person and trash or burn the letter. Writing helps to get rid of any negative suppressed emotions.

My prayer is that as I try my best to put some of my thoughts on paper, in book form, that God will allow me to help someone else find the Jesus that I love so much. He has been so good to me and after my experience of beating pancreatic cancer (having a one percent survival rate), along with three doctors giving me from two months to one and a half years to live, God has chosen to give me a clean bill of health.

It has always been my desire that the ministry God has allowed me to have would continue to live after I am gone. I am reminded of an old song that goes, somewhat, as follows:

Finding God: My Journey Through Pancreatic Cancer

If I can help somebody, as I pass along
If I can cheer somebody, with a word or song
If I can show somebody, that he's traveling wrong
Then my living shall not be in vain.

Chorus

My living shall not be in vain
Then my living shall not be in vain
If I can help somebody, as I pass along
Then my living shall not be in vain

If I can do my duty, as a good man ought
If I can bring back beauty, to a world up wrought
If I can spread love's message, as the Master taught
Then my living shall not be in vain.[15]

Congratulations on your new life. I pray that you have found God.

Blessings!

Endnotes

1   mayoclinic.org
2   Sinach, 2015
3   C. Austin Miles,1913
4   Mahalia Jackson
5   The Anointed Ones, Kenneth F. Haney, Radiant Life
Publications, 1992
6   Audrey Mieir, 1916-1996
7   Paul Rader, 1921
8   Notes found hand written by the author's mother with no
credit given for quotes and old hymns
9   Francis J. Crosby, 1882
10   A. A. Luther
11   Written by Sarah McCutcheon
12   (https://women.texaschildrens.org/program/texas-chil-
drens-fetal-center/conditions-wetreat/non-immune-hydrops)
13   (http://medlineplus.gov/ency/article/007308.htm)
14   Quote by Henry Ford
15   Written by Alma B. Androzzo (Published by Boosey and
Hawkes Ltd. 1945)